RENEWING ✛ WORSHIP

Congregational Song

Proposals for Renewal

Evangelical Lutheran Church in America
Published by Augsburg Fortress

RENEWING WORSHIP 1
Congregational Song: Proposals for Renewal

This resource has been prepared by the Evangelical Lutheran Church in America for provisional use.

Copyright © 2001 Evangelical Lutheran Church in America.

ACKNOWLEDGMENTS
ELCA staff—Division for Congregational Ministries and Publishing House: Ruth Allin, Kevin Anderson, Wyvetta Bullock, Michael Burk, Paul R. Nelson†, Linda Parriott, Michael Rothaar, Martin A. Seltz, Frank Stoldt, Karen Ward, Scott Weidler

Design and production: Eric Vollen, editorial production; Jürgen Selk, music engraving; Carolyn Porter of The Kantor Group, Inc., book design; Nicholas Markell, logo design

The paper used in this publication meets the minimum requirements of American National Standard for Information Sciences—Permanence of Paper for Printed Library Materials, ANSI Z329.48-1984.

Manufactured in the U.S.A.   ISBN 0-8066-7001-0

05 04 03 02 01   1 2 3 4 5

Preface

Welcome to Renewing Worship, a series of provisional resources prepared to encourage the exploration and evaluation of materials for worship in Lutheran churches.

In the years since the publication of *Lutheran Book of Worship* in 1978, the pace of change both within the church and beyond has quickened. The past three decades have seen not only a growing ecumenical consensus, but also a deepened focus on the church's mission to the world. The church has embraced broadened understandings of culture, increasing musical diversity, changes in the usage of language, a renewed understanding of the central pattern of Christian worship, and an explosion of electronic media and technologies. These shifts have had a profound effect on the weekly assembly gathered around word and sacrament. The present situation calls for a renewal of worship and of common resources for worship, a renewal grounded in the treasures of the church's history while open to the possibilities of the future.

Renewing Worship is a response to these emerging changes in the life of the church and the world. As the title of the series suggests, a principal goal of these resources is to provide worship leaders with a range of proposed strategies and materials that assist the renewal of corporate worship in a variety of settings. To that end, Renewing Worship offers provisional materials that address the various liturgical and musical needs of the church.

Published on a semi-annual basis beginning in 2001, this series includes hymns and songs (newly written or discovered as well as new approaches to common texts and tunes), liturgical texts and music for weekly and seasonal use, occasional rites (such as baptism, marriage, and burial), resources for daily prayer (morning prayer, evening prayer, and prayer at the close of the day), psalms and canticles, prayers and lectionary texts, and other supporting materials. Over the course of several years, worship leaders will have the opportunity to obtain and evaluate a wide range of Renewing Worship resources both in traditional print format and in electronic form delivered via the Internet (www.renewingworship.org).

The published resources of Renewing Worship, however, are only one component of a multi-year plan for worship. In fall 2000, the boards for the ELCA Division for Congregational Ministries and Augsburg Fortress, Publishers endorsed a plan for worship renewal that includes five components. The first phase (2001–2002) is a consultative process intended to develop principles for language and culture, music, worship space and environment, and preaching. Related to the ELCA's statement on sacramental practices, *The Use of the Means of Grace,* these newly developed *Principles for Worship* will serve to undergird future worship resource development and to encourage congregational practice.

The second phase (2001–2005) includes a series of working groups that will collect, develop, and revise worship materials based on *The Use of the Means of Grace* and *Principles for Worship.*

The liturgical and musical resource proposals that emerge from the working groups will be published during the third phase of this plan (also in 2001–2005) as trial-use resources in the Renewing Worship series. These materials will include proposals for newly developed, ecumenically shared, or recently revised texts, rites, and music. Crucial to this phase will be careful evaluation and response by congregations and worship leaders based on these proposed strategies and provisional materials.

The fourth phase of the plan includes regional conferences for conversation, resource introduction and evaluation, and congregational feedback. The final phase of the process (2005 and beyond) envisions the drafting of a comprehensive proposal for new primary worship resources designed to succeed *Lutheran Book of Worship.*

As the plan progresses, the shape and parameters of that proposal will continue to unfold. The goal, however, will remain constant: renewing the worship of God in the church as it carries out Christ's mission in a new day.

Introduction

The first Renewing Worship volume, *Congregational Song: Proposals for Renewal,* is focused on approaches to the renewal of the church's long heritage of congregational song. Future volumes in this series will contain proposals for recently written or newly collected hymns and songs.

Many texts and tunes are indelibly marked on the hearts and lips of individuals, as well as worshiping assemblies. Often these songs have served as foundations of faith and hope during transitions in the lives of people and communities. The church may best embrace these treasures by maintaining their continuity.

At other times, however, the song of the Christian assembly needs to be renewed if it is to be embraced by future generations of worshipers. The task of adaptation is not to be taken lightly; rather, the work of renewal requires careful consideration of various strategies and possibilities. Materials in this collection represent such a sampling of proposals.

The versions of hymns and songs in this resource are in no way a final recommendation for what may or may not be included in a future worship resource. Rather, these examples serve to demonstrate strategies for renewal and to elicit response and evaluation.

Renewal of Texts
Texts and translations of older hymns and songs may be enlivened by recovering biblical and poetic imagery included in original texts but obscured through centuries of revision. Often this can be accomplished by returning to older texts and gently revising them anew; at other times, new translations from original languages offer the greatest possibility for future use.

Another factor in revising texts is the memory of the worshiping assembly. The repeated experience of singing a specific version of a text or tune often makes revision difficult or suggests that an older version be restored in order to honor the memory of the assembly. In other cases, growing ecumenical awareness may lead to embracing versions of text or tune that are in widespread use among various communions of the Christian church.

An additional issue in textual revision is that of expansive language for God and humanity. Rather than limiting language, the biblical witness often unfolds a profoundly rich palette of images and words for God and this creation. Careful revision can balance archaic or gender-limited language with the richness of the church's tradition and with the reality of evolving meaning in any human language.

Renewal of hymn texts attends also to the correspondence of vowels, rhymes, and syllabic accents with the shape and meter of the musical setting. Some text and tune combinations are more successful than others in encouraging congregational singing.

Renewal of Music

The musical renewal of hymns and songs involves an equally challenging set of concerns. Gifted composers continue to generate new music worthy of learning. At other times, ecumenical convergence suggests the use of a tune or harmony held in common. The diversity of Christian communities across the globe presents new musical possibilities that offer a broader witness to the church's rich musical traditions. Finally, a pastoral need in certain circumstances for a more limited set of common tunes may require the availability of alternate tunes. In each case, the active participation of a worshiping assembly is the primary goal when making choices of tune and harmonization.

In *Congregational Song: Proposals for Renewal,* musical choices illustrate each of these possible strategies. Hymns best sung in unison have been included in melody-only versions; hymns intended for harmony singing have been included in versions that encourage congregational participation. A number of new text-tune combinations are suggested for use.

In the task of renewing hymns, a sense of balance among all the textual and musical concerns—memory, ecumenicity, expansiveness, imagery, musical shape, tune and harmony selection—is to be sought on a case-by-case basis.

Using This Resource

This collection is intended for provisional use among congregations of the Evangelical Lutheran Church in America and beyond. Worship leaders are encouraged to consider a congregation's history and musical repertoire before introducing new materials. Many hymns and songs in this volume can be used with a minimum of instruction; other selections, however, require careful introduction by cantors, choirs, or instrumentalists. In either case, congregations are more likely to embrace newer materials if they have been prepared for participation by their leaders.

Accompaniments have been included in this resource for all unison tunes that are not included in *Lutheran Book of Worship (LBW)*, *With One Voice (WOV)*, or *This Far by Faith (TFF)*. For other melodies included without accompaniment, references have been included to keyboard settings in *LBW, WOV,* or *TFF.*

Materials in this collection are intended for reproduction in congregational worship folders. Pages may be photocopied and trimmed for inclusion in orders of worship. Electronic graphic images of selected (but not all) materials are also available for download (www.renewingworship.org).

Questions of Copyright

Many of the texts and musical settings included in *Congregational Song: Proposals for Renewal* have no copyright restrictions and may be freely reproduced for inclusion in worship folders.

For materials in *Congregational Song: Proposals for Renewal* that are copyrighted and for which Augsburg Fortress serves as administrator, permission is granted to reproduce copies for local one-time, congregational use between July 1, 2001, and December 31, 2005. Information regarding this provision and the required copyright notice is included on page ii of this publication.

Other materials are administered by a variety of copyright holders and require additional permission for reproduction. It is the responsibility of the purchaser of this volume to obtain all required permissions, either through the purchase of appropriate copyright licenses or by requesting permission from the copyright holders. Accompanying each hymn is the information needed to fulfill this responsibility.

Evaluation

An essential goal of Renewing Worship is the evaluation of strategies and content proposals by worshiping congregations and their leaders. Included in each printed volume, as well as on the website (www.renewingworship.org), is a reproducible evaluation form that addresses the strategies employed in each volume of the series. Feedback received will help to shape the subsequent stages of the process toward new worship materials.

A Mighty Fortress Is Our God

1 A might-y for - tress is our God,
a sword and shield vic-to - rious,
who breaks the cruel op - pres - sor's rod
and wins sal - va - tion glo - rious.
The old e - vil foe, sworn to work us woe,
with guile and great might is armed to wage the fight:
on earth there is no e - qual.

2 No strength of ours can match this might!
We would be lost, re - ject - ed.
But now a cham - pion comes to fight,
whom God for us e - lect - ed.
Ask who this may be: Lord of hosts is he!
Christ Je - sus, our Lord, God's on - ly Son, a - dored,
shall hold the field vic - to - rious.

3 Though hordes of dev - ils fill the land
all threat - 'ning to de - vour us,
we trem - ble not, un - moved we stand;
they can - not o - ver - pow'r us.
And though Sa - tan rage, in fierce war en - gage,
this ty - rant shall fail; God's judg - ment must pre - vail!
One lit - tle word shall tri - umph.

4 The Word for - ev - er shall a - bide,
no thanks to foes, who fear it;
for God a - lone fights by our side
with weap - ons of the Spir - it.
If they take our house, goods, fame, child, or spouse,
wrench our life a - way, they can - not win the day.
The king - dom's ours for - ev - er!

Text: Martin Luther, 1483–1546; tr. *Lutheran Book of Worship*, alt.

Music: EIN FESTE BURG, Martin Luther, 1483–1546

Text © 1978 *Lutheran Book of Worship*, admin. Augsburg Fortress

This classic version of a Reformation hymn preserves the rhythmic vitality of music of the late Renaissance. The translation, prepared for *Lutheran Book of Worship* and subsequently adopted by other denominational worship books, is here adapted slightly to reduce gendered language. Martin Luther's original metaphor of Christian warfare against the power of evil remains integral to the hymn.—(Accompaniment: LBW 228)

A Mighty Fortress Is Our God

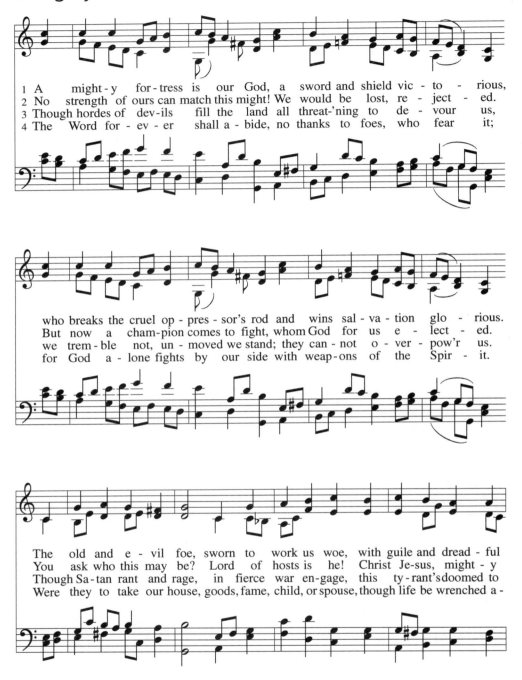

1 A might-y for-tress is our God, a sword and shield vic-to-rious,
2 No strength of ours can match this might! We would be lost, re-ject-ed.
3 Though hordes of dev-ils fill the land all threat-'ning to de-vour us,
4 The Word for-ev-er shall a-bide, no thanks to foes, who fear it;

who breaks the cruel op-pres-sor's rod and wins sal-va-tion glo-rious.
But now a cham-pion comes to fight, whom God for us e-lect-ed.
we trem-ble not, un-moved we stand; they can-not o-ver-pow'r us.
for God a-lone fights by our side with weap-ons of the Spir-it.

The old and e-vil foe, sworn to work us woe, with guile and dread-ful
You ask who this may be? Lord of hosts is he! Christ Je-sus, might-y
Though Sa-tan rant and rage, in fierce war en-gage, this ty-rant's doomed to
Were they to take our house, goods, fame, child, or spouse, though life be wrenched a-

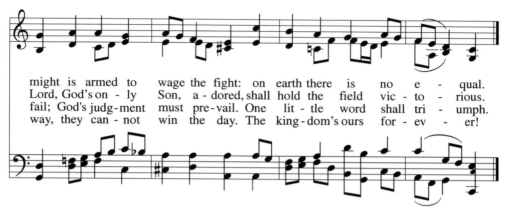

might is armed to   wage the fight: on earth there   is   no   e - qual.
Lord, God's on - ly   Son, a - dored, shall hold the   field   vic - to - rious.
fail; God's judg-ment must pre-vail. One lit - tle   word   shall tri - umph.
way, they can - not   win the day. The king-dom's ours for - ev - er!

Text: Martin Luther, 1483–1546; tr. *Lutheran Book of Worship,* alt.

Music: EIN FESTE BURG, Martin Luther, 1483–1546; arr. J.S. Bach, 1685–1750

Text © 1978 *Lutheran Book of Worship,* admin. Augsburg Fortress

In the two hundred years after its introduction, the tune EIN FESTE BURG was increasingly sung in an isometric version; that is, a version in which syncopated rhythms are evened out using equal note values. The harmonizations of J.S. Bach, including this one from Cantata 80, illustrate this approach. It may be sung in alternation with the rhythmic version above.

A Stable Lamp Is Lighted

1 A sta - ble lamp is light - ed whose
2 (This) child through Da - vid's cit - y shall
3 (Yet) he shall be for - sak - en and
4 (But) now, as at the end - ing, the

glow shall wake the sky; the stars shall bend their voic - es, and
ride in tri - umph by; the palm shall strew its branch - es, and
yield - ed up to die; the sky shall groan and dark - en, and
low is lift - ed high; the stars shall bend their voic - es, and

ev - 'ry stone shall cry. And ev - 'ry stone shall
ev - 'ry stone shall cry. And ev - 'ry stone shall
ev - 'ry stone shall cry. And ev - 'ry stone shall
ev - 'ry stone shall cry. And ev - 'ry stone shall

cry, and straw like gold shall shine; a barn shall har - bor
cry though heav - y, dull, and dumb, and lie with - in the
cry for ston - y hearts of men: God's blood up - on the
cry in prais - es of the child by whose de - scent a -

heav - en, a stall be - come a shrine.
road - way to pave his king - dom come.
spear - head, God's love re - fused a - gain.
mong us the worlds are rec - on - ciled.

1–3

4

2 This
3 Yet
4 But

1–3

4

Text: Richard Wilbur, b. 1921

Music: ANDUJAR, David Hurd, b. 1950

Text © 1961, 1989 Richard Wilbur, admin. Harcourt Brace Jovanovich, Inc., 6277 Sea Harbor Dr., Orlando FL 32887, (407) 345-3575

Music © 1984 GIA Publications Inc., 7404 S. Mason Ave., Chicago IL 60638, (800) 442-1358. All rights reserved.

This Christmas hymn by one of the leading twentieth century poets in the United States, which appeared in *Lutheran Book of Worship* to a different tune, has often been paired with this melody by David Hurd.

A Stable Lamp Is Lighted

1 A sta - ble lamp is light - ed whose glow shall wake the sky;
2 This child through Da - vid's cit - y shall ride in tri - umph by;
3 Yet he shall be for - sak - en, and yield - ed up to die;
4 But now, as at the end - ing, the low is lift - ed high;

the stars shall bend their voic - es, and ev - 'ry stone shall cry.
the palm shall strew its branch - es, and ev - 'ry stone shall cry.
the sky shall groan and dark - en, and ev - 'ry stone shall cry.
the stars shall bend their voic - es, and ev - 'ry stone shall cry.

And ev - 'ry stone shall cry, and straw like gold shall shine;
And ev - 'ry stone shall cry though heav - y, dull, and dumb,
And ev - 'ry stone shall cry for ston - y hearts of men:
And ev - 'ry stone shall cry in prais - es of the child

a barn shall har - bor heav - en, a stall be - come a shrine.
and lie with - in the road - way to pave his king - dom come.
God's blood up - on the spear - head, God's love re - fused a - gain.
by whose de - scent a - mong us the worlds are rec - on - ciled.

Text: Richard Wilbur, b. 1921

Music: ANDUJAR, David Hurd, b. 1950

Text © 1961, 1989 Richard Wilbur, admin. Harcourt Brace Jovanovich, Inc., 6277 Sea Harbor Dr., Orlando FL 32887, (407) 345-3575

Music © 1984 GIA Publications Inc., 7404 S. Mason Ave., Chicago IL 60638, (800) 442-1358. All rights reserved.

This Christmas hymn by one of the leading twentieth century poets in the United States, which appeared in *Lutheran Book of Worship* to a different tune, has often been paired with this melody by David Hurd.—(Accompaniment: page 4)

Ah, Holy Jesus

1 Ah, ho-ly Je-sus, how have you of-fend-ed that mor-tal
2 Who was the guilt-y? Who brought this up-on you? A-las, my
3 Lo, the Good Shep-herd for the sheep is of-fered; the slave has
4 For me, kind Je-sus, was your in-car-na-tion, your mor-tal
5 There-fore, kind Je-sus, since I can-not pay you, I do a-

judg-ment has on you de-scend-ed? By foes de-rid-ed,
trea-son, Je-sus, has un-done you. 'Twas I, Lord Je-sus,
sin-ned, and the Son has suf-fered; for our a-tone-ment,
sor-row, and your life's ob-la-tion; your death of an-guish
dore you, and will ev-er pray you; think on your pit-y

by your own re-ject-ed, O most af-flict-ed.
I it was de-nied you; I cru-ci-fied you.
while we noth-ing heed-ed, God in-ter-ced-ed.
and your bit-ter pas-sion, for my sal-va-tion.
and your love un-swerv-ing, not my de-serv-ing.

Text: Johann Heermann, 1585–1647; tr. Robert Bridges, 1844–1930, alt.
Music: HERZLIEBSTER JESU, Johann Crüger, 1598–1662

Robert Bridges' translation of this chorale has been sung for over a century during Lent and Holy Week. Updating of archaic language has been applied to this hymn, a deeply personal appropriation of the passion of Jesus Christ.—(Accompaniment: LBW 123)

All Creatures, Worship God Most High!

1 All creatures, worship God most high! Sound ev - 'ry voice in
2 Sing, broth - er wind; with clouds and rain you grow the gifts of
3 O fire, our broth - er, mirth - ful, strong, drive far the shad - ows,
4 All who for love of God for - give, all who in pain or

earth and sky: Al - le - lu - ia! Al - le - lu - ia!
fruit and grain: Al - le - lu - ia! Al - le - lu - ia!
join the throng: Al - le - lu - ia! Al - le - lu - ia!
sor - row grieve: Al - le - lu - ia! Al - le - lu - ia!

Sing, broth - er sun, in splen - dor bright; sing, sis - ter moon
Dear sis - ter wa - ter, use - ful, clear, make mu - sic for
O earth, our moth - er, rich in care, praise God in col -
Christ bears your bur - dens and your fears; still make your song

Refrain

and stars of night: your Lord to hear: Al - le - lu - ia, al - le - lu - ia,
your Lord to hear:
ors bright and rare:
a - mid the tears:

al - le - lu - ia, al - le - lu - ia, al - le - lu - ia!

5 Come, sister death, your song release
   when you enfold our breath in peace: Alleluia! Alleluia!
   Since Christ our light has pierced your gloom,
   fair is the night that leads us home. *Refrain*

6 O sisters, brothers, take your part,
   and worship God with humble heart: Alleluia! Alleluia!
   All creatures, bless the Father, Son,
   and Holy Spirit, Three in One: *Refrain*

Text: attr. Francis of Assisi, 1182–1226; tr. Martin A. Seltz, b. 1951

Music: LASST UNS ERFREUEN, *Geistliche Kirchengesänge*, Köln, 1623

Text © 1999 Augsburg Fortress

Permission is granted for congregations to reproduce this hymn between July 1, 2001, and December 31, 2005, provided copies are for local use only and the following copyright notice appears: From *Congregational Song: Proposals for Renewal*, © 2001, admin. Augsburg Fortress.

This "Canticle of the Sun" is attributed to Francis of Assisi, well known for his care for the created order. This version of Francis's song closely reflects the original language inviting sisters and brothers in all creation to a cosmic alleluia.
—(Accompaniment: LBW 527)

All My Heart This Night Rejoices

1 All my heart this night rejoic - es as I hear, far and
2 Hark! A voice from yon-der man - ger, soft and sweet, does en -
3 Come, then, let us has-ten yon - der; here let all, great and
4 You, dear Lord, I'll ev - er cher - ish; though my breath fail in

near, sweet-est an - gel voic - es; "Christ is born," their choirs are
treat, "Flee from woe and dan - ger; come and see; from all that
small, kneel in awe and won - der; love him who with love is
death, I will nev - er per - ish: by your side in light e -

sing - ing, till the air ev - 'ry - where now with joy is ring - ing.
grieves you you are freed; all you need I will sure-ly give you."
yearn - ing; hail the star that from far bright with hope is burn - ing.
ter - nal I shall be end-less - ly filled with joy su - per - nal.

Text: Paul Gerhardt, 1607–1676; tr. Catherine Winkworth, 1829–1878, alt.

Music: WARUM SOLLT ICH, Johann Georg Ebeling, 1637–1676

Paul Gerhardt's Christmas hymn is associated with several different tunes, including the one in *Lutheran Book of Worship* (no. 46). This alternate tune by Johann Ebeling appeared in *Service Book and Hymnal* (1958). An additional stanza of the original fifteen and Winkworth's familiar title have also been restored.

Alleluia! Lord and Savior

Al - le - lu - ia! Lord and Sav - ior: o - pen now your sav - ing Word.

Let it burn like fire with - in us; speak un - til our hearts are stirred.

Al - le - lu - ia! Lord, we sing for the good news that you bring.

Text: metrical gospel acclamation, Gracia Grindal, b. 1943

Music: UNSER HERRSCHER, Joachim Neander, 1650–1680

Text © 1998 Augsburg Fortress

Precedent for metrical paraphrases of liturgical texts reaches back before the Reformation to the medieval *leisen*. This text was part of a hymn mass commissioned for *Sundays and Seasons*. Paraphrases of the principal recurring portions of the eucharistic liturgy comprise the hymn mass texts, which can be sung to a variety of common tunes.—(Accompaniment: LBW 250)

Amazing Grace, How Sweet the Sound

1 A - maz - ing grace, how sweet the sound, that
2 'Twas grace that taught my heart to fear, and
3 Through man - y dan - gers, toils, and snares I
4 The Lord has prom - ised good to me; his

saved a wretch like me! I once was lost, but
grace my fears re - lieved; how pre - cious did that
have al - read - y come; 'tis grace has brought me
word my hope se - cures; he will my shield and

now am found; was blind, but now I see.
grace ap - pear the hour I first be - lieved!
safe thus far, and grace will lead me home.
por - tion be as long as life en - dures.

Text: John Newton, 1725–1807
Music: NEW BRITAIN, W. Walker, *Southern Harmony*, 1835

One of the most beloved hymns in the English language, the former slave trader John Newton's testimony to God's grace is here presented with a common harmonization suitable for four-part singing.

As Saints of Old

1 As saints of old their first-fruits brought of or-chard, flock, and field
2 A world in need now sum-mons us to la-bor, love, and give;
3 In grat-i-tude and hum-ble trust we bring our best to-day

to God, the giv-er of all good, the source of boun-teous yield;
to make our life an of-fer-ing to God, that all may live.
to serve your cause and share your love with all a-long life's way.

so we to-day first-fruits would bring, the wealth of this good land,
The church of Christ is call-ing us to make the dream come true:
O God, who gave your-self to us in Je-sus Christ your Son,

of farm and mar-ket, shop and home, of mind and heart and hand.
a world re-deemed by Christ-like love; all life in Christ made new.
teach us to give our-selves each day un-til life's work is done.

Text: Frank von Christierson, 1900–1996
Music: FOREST GREEN, English folk tune

Frank von Christierson's fine stewardship hymn was one of ten commissioned by the Hymn Society and published in 1961.
Pairing it with FOREST GREEN, an English folk melody in an easily remembered AABA form, may serve to broaden its use.
—(Accompaniment: WOV 725)

Behold a Host

1 Be - hold a host, ar - rayed in white, like thou-sand snow - clad
2 De - spised and scorned they so - journed here; but now, how glo - rious
3 Then hail! ye might - y le - gions, yea, all hail! now safe and

moun-tains bright, with palms they stand. Who is this band
they ap - pear! Those mar - tyrs stand, a priest - ly band,
blest for aye; and praise the Lord, who with his word

be - fore the throne of light? Lo, these are they of glo - rious fame
God's throne for - ev - er near. So oft, in trou-bled days gone by,
sus - tained you on the way. Ye did the joys of earth dis - dain,

who from the great af - flic - tion came and in the flood of
in an - guish they would weep and sigh; at home a - bove the
ye toiled and sowed in tears and pain; fare - well, now bring your

Je - sus' blood are cleansed from guilt and blame.
God of love for aye their tears shall dry.
sheaves and sing sal - va - tion's glad re - frain.

Now gath-ered in the ho - ly place, their voic - es they in
They now en - joy their sab - bath rest, the pas - chal ban - quet
Swing high your palms, lift up your song, yea, make it myr - iad

wor - ship raise, their an - thems swell where
of the blest; the Lamb, their Lord, at
voic - es strong. E - ter - nal - ly shall

God doth dwell 'mid an - gels' songs of praise.
fes - tal board him - self is host and guest.
praise to thee, God, and the Lamb be - long.

Text: Hans A. Brorson, 1694–1764; tr. composite

Music: DEN STORE HVIDE FLOK, Norwegian folk tune, 17th cent.

Should an earlier and possibly more archaic version of a hymn sometimes be restored because of its connection to the memories of worshipers? This classic translation of Hans Brorson's hymn based on Revelation 7 may be an example.
—(Accompaniment: LBW 314)

Bread of the World, in Mercy Broken

Bread of the world, in mer-cy bro-ken, Wine of the soul, in
mer-cy shed, by whom the words of life were spo-ken, and
in whose death our sins are dead: look on the heart by sor-row
bro-ken, look on the tears by sin-ners shed; and be thy
feast to us the to-ken that by thy grace our souls are fed.

Text: Reginald Heber, 1783–1826
Music: RENDEZ À DIEU, attr. Louis Bourgeois, c. 1510–1561

The songs of Taizé, such as "Jesus, remember me," have illustrated the strength of a genre of songs that bear repetition and can become songs of the heart. Such songs are especially useful when people are moving to receive communion. This text, set to a French psalm tune, may be used in a similar way. The hymn may also be used as an alternative to "Lamb of God" at the breaking of the bread.—(Accompaniment: WOV 704)

Christ Is Alive! Let Christians Sing

1 Christ is a - live! Let Chris - tians sing. The cross stands
2 Christ is a - live! No long - er bound to dis - tant
3 In ev - 'ry in - sult, rift, and war, where col - or,
4 Wom - en and men, in age and youth, can feel the
5 Christ is a - live, and comes to bring good news to

emp - ty to the sky. Let streets and homes with
years in Pal - es - tine, but sav - ing, hea - ling,
scorn, or wealth di - vide, Christ suf - fers still, yet
Spir - it, hear the call, and find the life, the
this and ev - 'ry age, till earth and sky and

prais - es ring. Love, drowned in death, shall nev - er die.
here and now, and touch - ing ev - 'ry place and time.
loves the more, and lives, where e - ven hope has died.
way, the truth, re - vealed in Je - sus, freed for all.
o - cean ring with joy, with jus - tice, love, and praise.

Text: Brian Wren, b. 1936

Music: TRURO, T. Williams, *Psalmodia Evangelica*, 1789

Text © 1975, 1995 Hope Publishing Co., 380 S. Main Pl., Carol Stream IL 60188, (800) 323-1049. All rights reserved.

Duplication in any form prohibited without permission or valid license from copyright administrator.

Language and its meanings have seemed to evolve at a more rapid pace over the past generation. Brian Wren is one poet who has taken to heart this progression and revised his own work in response. This is the author's revision of a text that appeared in *Lutheran Book of Worship*.—(Accompaniment: LBW 363)

Christ Is Risen! Shout Hosanna

1 Christ is ris - en! Shout ho - san - na! Cel - e - brate this day of days!
2 Christ is ris - en! Raise your spir - its from the cav - erns of de - spair.
3 Christ is ris - en! Earth and heav - en nev - er - more shall be the same.

Christ is ris - en! Hush in won - der: all cre - a - tion is a - mazed.
Walk with glad - ness in the morn - ing. See what love can do and dare.
Break the bread of new cre - a - tion where the world is still in pain.

In the des - ert all sur - round - ing, see, a spread - ing tree has grown.
Drink the wine of res - ur - rec - tion. Not a ser - vant, but a friend,
Tell its grim, de - mon - ic chor - us: "Christ is ris - en! Get you gone!"

Heal - ing leaves of grace a - bound - ing bring a taste of love un - known.
Je - sus is our strong com - pan - ion. Joy and peace shall nev - er end.
God the first and last is with us. Sing ho - san - na, ev - 'ry - one!

Text: Brian Wren, b. 1936
Music: AUSTRIA, Franz Joseph Hadyn, 1732–1809

16   Another Brian Wren text, which appears in *With One Voice* with the jazzy tune JACKSON NEW, is here paired with a sturdy older tune. What is a helpful balance between new tunes and old favorites? How does the context in which they are sung affect the answer to this question?—(Accompaniment: LBW 540)

Christ Is the King!

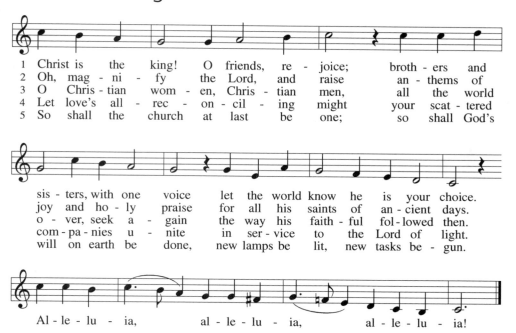

1 Christ is the king! O friends, re - joice; broth - ers and
2 Oh, mag - ni - fy the Lord, and raise an - thems of
3 O Chris - tian wom - en, Chris - tian men, all the world
4 Let love's all - rec - on - cil - ing might your scat - tered
5 So shall the church at last be one; so shall God's

sis - ters, with one voice let the world know he is your choice.
joy and ho - ly praise for all his saints of an - cient days.
o - ver, seek a - gain the way his faith - ful fol - lowed then.
com - pa - nies u - nite in ser - vice to the Lord of light.
will on earth be done, new lamps be lit, new tasks be - gun.

Al - le - lu - ia, al - le - lu - ia, al - le - lu - ia!

Text: George K. A. Bell, 1883–1958, alt.

Music: GELOBT SEI GOTT, Melchior Vulpius, c. 1570–1615

Here is another example of the pairing of a relatively new text, celebrating the reign of Christ, with an alternate tune. This tune is no less energetic than the one in *Lutheran Book of Worship* but has a longer history of use.—(Accompaniment: LBW 144)

Christ, Mighty Savior

1 Christ, might-y Sav-ior, Light of all cre-a-tion, you make the
2 Now comes the day's end as the sun is set-ting: mir-ror of
3 There-fore we come now eve-ning rites to of-fer, joy-ful-ly
4 Give heed, we pray you, to our sup-pli-ca-tion: that you may
5 Though bod-ies slum-ber, hearts shall keep their vig-il, for-ev-er

day-time ra-diant with the sun-light and to the night give
day-break, pledge of res-ur-rec-tion; while in the heav-ens
chant-ing ho-ly hymns to praise you, with all cre-a-tion
grant us par-don for of-fens-es, strength for our weak hearts,
rest-ing in the peace of Je-sus, in light or dark-ness

glit-ter-ing a-dorn-ment, stars in the heav-ens.
choirs of stars ap-pear-ing hal-low the night-fall.
join-ing hearts and voic-es, sing-ing your glo-ry.
rest for ach-ing bod-ies, sooth-ing the wea-ry.
wor-ship-ing our Sav-ior now and for-ev-er.

Text: Mozarabic, 10th cent.; tr. Alan McDougall, 1895–1964 and Anne LeCroy, b. 1930

Music: MIGHTY SAVIOR, David Hurd, b. 1950

Christ, Mighty Savior

1 Christ, might - y Sav - ior, Light of all cre - a - tion, you make the
2 Now comes the day's end as the sun is set - ting: mir - ror of
3 There - fore we come now eve - ning rites to of - fer, joy - ful - ly
4 Give heed, we pray you, to our sup - pli - ca - tion: that you may
5 Though bod - ies slum - ber, hearts shall keep their vig - il, for - ev - er

day - time ra - diant with the sun - light and to the night give
day - break, pledge of res - ur - rec - tion; while in the heav - ens
chant - ing ho - ly hymns to praise you, with all cre - a - tion
grant us par - don for of - fens - es, strength for our weak hearts,
rest - ing in the peace of Je - sus, in light or dark - ness

glit - ter - ing a - dorn - ment, stars in the heav - ens.
choirs of stars ap - pear - ing hal - low the night - fall.
join - ing hearts and voic - es, sing - ing your glo - ry.
rest for ach - ing bod - ies, sooth - ing the wea - ry.
wor - ship - ing our Sav - ior now and for - ev - er.

Text: Mozarabic, 10th cent.; tr. Alan McDougall, 1895–1964 and Anne LeCroy, b. 1930
Music: MIGHTY SAVIOR, David Hurd, b. 1950

A rich hymn text for evening from the Mozarabic tradition of Spain is here paired with a tune by David Hurd that enjoys ecumenical use alongside the tune INNISFREE FARM, which was used in *With One Voice*.

Come, Lord Jesus

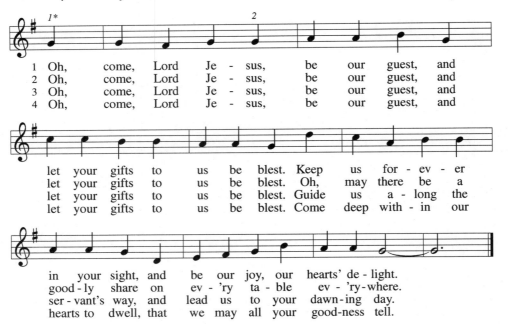

1 Oh, come, Lord Je - sus, be our guest, and
2 Oh, come, Lord Je - sus, be our guest, and
3 Oh, come, Lord Je - sus, be our guest, and
4 Oh, come, Lord Je - sus, be our guest, and

let your gifts to us be blest. Keep us for - ev - er
let your gifts to us be blest. Oh, may there be a
let your gifts to us be blest. Guide us a - long the
let your gifts to us be blest. Come deep with - in our

in your sight, and be our joy, our hearts' de - light.
good - ly share on ev - 'ry ta - ble ev - 'ry-where.
ser - vant's way, and lead us to your dawn-ing day.
hearts to dwell, that we may all your good-ness tell.

*may be sung in canon

Text: traditional table prayer, adapt. Susan Briehl
Music: TALLIS' CANON, Thomas Tallis
Text © 1996 Augsburg Fortress

Permission is granted for congregations to reproduce this hymn between July 1, 2001, and December 31, 2005, provided copies are for local use only and the following copyright notice appears: From *Congregational Song: Proposals for Renewal*, © 2001, admin. Augsburg Fortress.

A common table prayer that may have originated in nineteenth century Germany was paraphrased and expanded by Susan Briehl in the devotional booklet *Come, Lord Jesus* and further adapted for singing in *LifeSongs*. Useful in the home, the expanded text may also find a place in parish gatherings and the worshiping assembly, especially during Advent.
—(Accompaniment: LBW 278)

Come, Thou Long-Expected Jesus

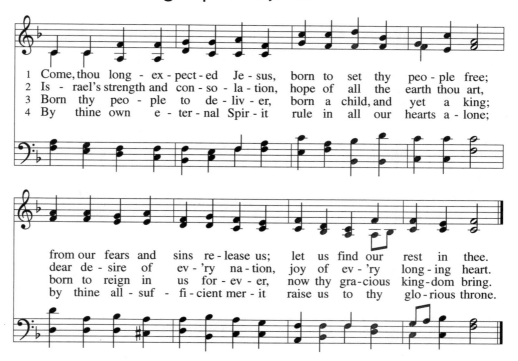

1 Come, thou long - ex - pect - ed Je - sus, born to set thy peo - ple free;
2 Is - rael's strength and con - so - la - tion, hope of all the earth thou art,
3 Born thy peo - ple to de - liv - er, born a child, and yet a king;
4 By thine own e - ter - nal Spir - it rule in all our hearts a - lone;

from our fears and sins re - lease us; let us find our rest in thee.
dear de - sire of ev - 'ry na - tion, joy of ev - 'ry long - ing heart.
born to reign in us for - ev - er, now thy gra - cious king - dom bring.
by thine all - suf - fi - cient mer - it raise us to thy glo - rious throne.

Text: Charles Wesley, 1707–1788
Music: STUTTGART, Christian Friedrich Witt, 1660–1716

This combination of tune and text has wide ecumenical use and is suitable for four-part singing. For songs that are arranged to be sung in harmony, when is it helpful to encourage singing in parts? When might part singing divide the assembly and intimidate the less musically inclined?

Creator of the Stars of Night

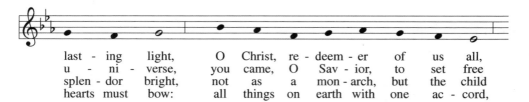

1 Cre - a - tor of the stars of night, your peo - ple's ev - er -
2 In sor - row that the an - cient curse should doom to death a
3 When this old world drew on toward night, you came; but not in
4 At your great name, O Je - sus, now all knees must bend, all

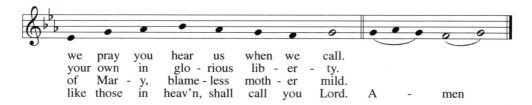

last - ing light, O Christ, re - deem - er of us all,
u - ni - verse, you came, O Sav - ior, to set free
splen - dor bright, not as a mon - arch, but the child
hearts must bow: all things on earth with one ac - cord,

we pray you hear us when we call.
your own in glo - rious lib - er - ty.
of Mar - y, blame - less moth - er mild.
like those in heav'n, shall call you Lord. A - men

5 Come in your holy might, we pray,
redeem us for eternal day;
defend us while we dwell below
from all assaults of our dread foe.

6 To God the Father, God the Son,
and God the Spirit, Three in One,
praise, honor, might, and glory be
from age to age eternally. Amen

Text: Latin, 9th cent.; versification *Hymnal 1940*, alt.

Music: Conditor alme siderum, plainsong, mode 1

Text © 1940 Church Pension Fund, admin. Church Publishing Inc., 445 Fifth Ave., New York NY 10016, (800) 223-6602.

This ancient, yearning Advent hymn, which appears in *Lutheran Book of Worship* with a different translation, is here presented with a text version that enjoys broad ecumenical use. Stemless notation is used to communicate the free, unmetered flow of chant.—(Accompaniment: LBW 323)

Cup of Blessing That We Share

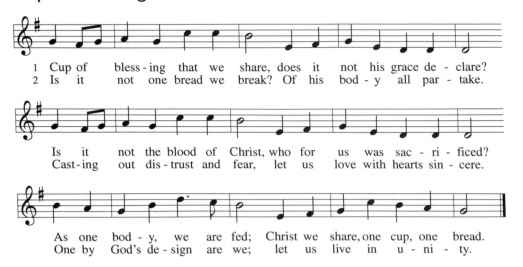

1 Cup of bless-ing that we share, does it not his grace de - clare?
2 Is it not one bread we break? Of his bod - y all par - take.

Is it not the blood of Christ, who for us was sac - ri - ficed?
Cast-ing out dis - trust and fear, let us love with hearts sin - cere.

As one bod - y, we are fed; Christ we share, one cup, one bread.
One by God's de - sign are we; let us live in u - ni - ty.

Text: Bernard Mischke, b. 1926, alt.

Music: Dix, Conrad Kocher, 1786–1872

A widely used hymn tune is here matched with a eucharistic hymn text based on 1 Corinthians 10.—(Accompaniment: LBW 561)

Day of Arising

1 Day of a - ris - ing, Christ on the road - way,
2 When we are walk - ing, doubt - ful and dread - ing,
3 Lo, I am with you, Je - sus has spo - ken.
4 Christ, our com - pan - ion, hope for the jour - ney,

un - known com - pan - ion walks with his own.
blind - ed by sad - ness, slow - ness of heart,
This is Christ's prom - ise, this is Christ's sign:
bread of com - pas - sion, o - pen our eyes.

When they in - vite him, as fades the first day,
yet Christ walks with us ev - er a - wait - ing
when the church gath - ers, when bread is bro - ken,
Grant us your vi - sion, set all hearts burn - ing

and bread is bro - ken, Christ is made known.
our in - vi - ta - tion: Stay, do not part.
there Christ is with us in bread and wine.
that all cre - a - tion with you may rise.

Text: Susan Palo Cherwien, b. 1953

Music: BUNESSAN, Gaelic melody

Text © 1996 Susan Palo Cherwien, admin. Augsburg Fortress

This folk melody, popularized by its association with "Morning has broken," is here combined with a new text for the Easter season which recalls the encounter of the risen Christ with the disciples on the road to Emmaus.—(Accompaniment: LBW 409, WOV 693)

Deep River

Refrain

Deep riv-er, my home is o-ver Jor-dan,
deep riv-er, Lord, I want to cross o-ver in-to camp-ground.

1 Oh, don't you want to go to that gos-pel feast,
2 Oh, when I get to heav-en, I'll . . . take my seat,

that prom-ised land where all is peace? Oh,
and cast my crown at Je-sus' feet. Oh,

Refrain

Text: African American spiritual

Music: DEEP RIVER, African American spiritual

A renewed repertoire of hymns will incorporate the treasures of various cultural and ethnic traditions that have gained wider use in recent years. "Deep river" resonates not only with the African American experience but with rich sacramental associations.—(Accompaniment: TFF 174)

Faith of Our Fathers

1 Faith of our fa - thers, liv - ing still in spite of dun - geon,
2 Faith of our moth - ers, dar - ing faith, your work for Christ is
3 Faith of our sis - ters, broth - ers too, who still must bear op -
4 Faith born of God, oh, call us yet, bind us with all who

fire, and sword. Oh, how our hearts beat high with joy
love re - vealed, spread-ing God's word from pole to pole,
pres - sion's might, rais - ing on high, in pris - ons dark,
fol - low you, shar - ing the strug - gle of your cross

when-e'er we hear that glo - rious word. Faith of our fa - thers,
mak - ing love known and free - dom real. Faith of our mo - thers,
the cross of Christ still burn - ing bright. Faith for to - day, O
un - til the world is made a - new. Faith born of God, O

ho - ly faith, we will be true to you till death.
ho - ly faith, we will be true to you till death.
liv - ing faith, we will be true to you till death.
liv - ing faith, we will be true to you till death.

Text: Frederick W. Faber, 1814–1863, alt., st. 1; Joseph R. Alfred, b. 1947, sts. 2–4
Music: ST. CATHERINE, Henri F. Hemy, 1818–1888; James G. Walton, 1821–1905, refrain
Text sts. 2–4 © Joseph R. Alfred, 9825 S. Campbell Ave., Evergreen Park, IL 60805

One approach to revising well-known hymns with gendered language is to combine older and newer texts in balance. This version of a beloved hymn, from the United Church of Canada's recent worship book *Voices United,* illustrates this strategy.—(Accompaniment: LBW 500)

For Perfect Love So Freely Spent

1 For per-fect love so free-ly spent, for fel-low-ship re - stored,
2 We come, by sin dis-qui-et-ed, and find our lives made whole;
3 A - bide with us; in all our ways your sav-ing love be shown;

we cel - e - brate your sac - ra - ment and sing your praise, O Lord.
a - round this ta - ble we are fed re - fresh-ment for the soul.
so may our lives be hymns of praise, O Christ, to you a - lone.

Text: Louise M. McDowell, b. 1923

Music: LAND OF REST, North American

Text © 1972 The Westminster Press, admin. Presbyterian Publishing Corp., 100 S. Witherspoon St., Louisville KY 40202, (502) 569-5060.

Lutheran Book of Worship included a number of newer hymns exploring images of holy communion that were less prominent in earlier hymns. Here is one example, paired with a frequently sung North American folk melody.
—(Accompaniment: LBW 331)

For the Bread Which You Have Broken

1 For the bread which you have bro-ken, for the wine which you have poured,
2 By this prom-ise that you love us, by your gift of peace re-stored,
3 With the saints who now a-dore you seat-ed at our Fa-ther's board,
4 In your ser-vice, Lord, de-fend us; in our hearts keep watch and ward,

for the words which you have spo-ken, now we give you thanks, O Lord.
by your call to heav'n a-bove us, hal-low all our lives, O Lord.
may the church still wait-ing for you keep love's tie un-bro-ken, Lord.
in the world to which you send us let your king-dom come, O Lord.

Text: Louis E. Benson, 1885–1930, alt.

Music: BENG LI, I-to Loh, b. 1936

Text © 1924 Louis E. Benson, admin. Robert Jeffreys Jr., 375 Weadley Rd., King of Prussia PA 19406.

Music © 1983 The United Methodist Publishing House, admin. The Copyright Company, 40 Music Square E., Nashville TN 37203, (615) 244-5588. All rights reserved.

28   In the past generation, churches throughout the world have become more aware of the gifts of song they have to offer one another. This combination of a text from North America with a tune by a Taiwanese composer illustrates one approach to cross-cultural sharing of these gifts.

From God the Father, Virgin-Born

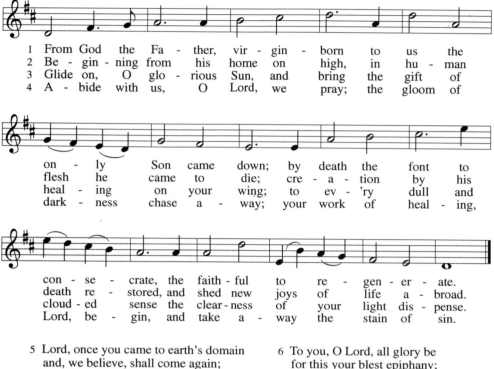

1 From God the Fa - ther, vir - gin - born to us the
2 Be - gin - ning from his home on high, in hu - man
3 Glide on, O glo - rious Sun, and bring the gift of
4 A - bide with us, O Lord, we pray; the gloom of

on - ly Son came down; by death the font to
flesh he came to die; cre - a - tion by his
heal - ing on your wing; to ev - 'ry dull and
dark - ness chase a - way; your work of heal - ing,

con - se - crate, the faith - ful to re - gen - er - ate.
death re - stored, and shed new joys of life a - broad.
cloud - ed sense the clear - ness of your light dis - pense.
Lord, be - gin, and take a - way the stain of sin.

5 Lord, once you came to earth's domain
and, we believe, shall come again;
be with us on the battlefield,
from ev'ry harm your people shield.

6 To you, O Lord, all glory be
for this your blest epiphany;
to God whom all his hosts adore,
and Holy Spirit evermore.

Text: Latin office hymn, c. 11th cent.; tr. John M. Neale, 1818–1866, alt.
Music: TRURO, T. Williams, *Psalmodia Evangelica*, 1789

A thousand years old, this hymn text celebrating the baptism of Jesus may be sung to this tune as an alternate to the one in *Lutheran Book of Worship.*—(Accompaniment: LBW 363)

From Heaven Above

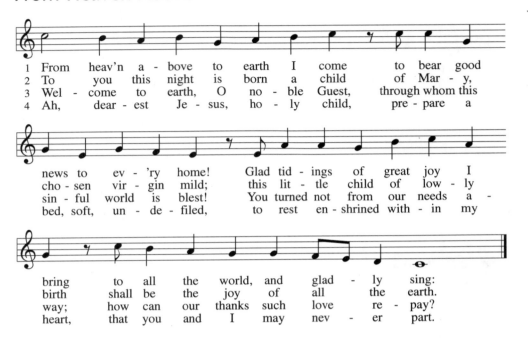

1. From heav'n a-bove to earth I come to bear good
2. To you this night is born a child of Mar-y,
3. Wel-come to earth, O no-ble Guest, through whom this
4. Ah, dear-est Je-sus, ho-ly child, pre-pare a

news to ev-'ry home! Glad tid-ings of great joy I
cho-sen vir-gin mild; this lit-tle child of low-ly
sin-ful world is blest! You turned not from our needs a-
bed, soft, un-de-filed, to rest en-shrined with-in my

bring to all the world, and glad-ly sing:
birth shall be the joy of all the earth.
way; how can our thanks such love re-pay?
heart, that you and I may nev-er part.

5 My heart for very joy now leaps;
my voice no longer silence keeps;
I too must sing with joyful tongue
the sweetest ancient cradle-song:

6 "Glory to God in highest heaven,
who unto us a Son has given."
With angels sing in pious mirth
a glad new year to all the earth!

Text: Martin Luther, 1483–1546; tr. Catherine Winkworth, alt.
Music: VOM HIMMEL HOCH, V. Schumann, *Geistliche Lieder,* 1539

Luther wrote a ballad telling the Christmas story for his family's Christmas Eve celebration, setting it to the tune of a current folk song. Later it was combined with this tune, which may be from Luther's own hand. This version is abridged from the original fifteen stanzas.—(Accompaniment: LBW 51)

Glory Be to God in Heaven

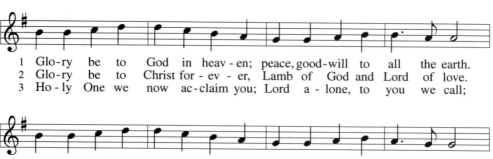

1 Glo-ry be to God in heav - en; peace, good-will to all the earth.
2 Glo-ry be to Christ for - ev - er, Lamb of God and Lord of love.
3 Ho - ly One we now ac-claim you; Lord a - lone, to you we call;

Might-y God of all cre - a - tion, Fa - ther of sur - pass - ing worth:
Son of God and gra-cious Sav - ior, you have come from heav'n a - bove;
Ho - ly One in faith we name you, throned on high, yet near to all:

we ex - alt you, we a - dore you, we lift high our thanks and praise.
on the cross you died to save us; now you reign at God's right hand.
Je - sus Christ, with God the Spir - it, in the Fa - ther's splen - dor bright.

Saints and an - gels bow be - fore you; here on earth our songs we raise.
Hear our prayer; re - store, for - give us; in your prom-ise firm we stand.
For the peace that we in - her - it, glo - ry be to God on high!

Text: metrical Gloria in excelsis, Martin A. Seltz, b. 1951
Music: HYMN TO JOY, Ludwig van Beethoven, 1770–1827, adapt.
Text © 1998 Augsburg Fortress

Precedent for metrical paraphrases of liturgical texts reaches back before the Reformation to the medieval *leisen*. This text was part of a hymn mass commissioned for *Sundays and Seasons*. Paraphrases of the principal recurring portions of the eucharistic liturgy comprise the hymn mass texts, which can be sung to a variety of common tunes.—(Accompaniment: LBW 551)

God Is Truly Present

1 God is tru-ly pres-ent; let us come a-dor-ing and with awe our
2 God is tru-ly pres-ent; hear the harps re-sound-ing; see the hosts the
3 Light of light e-ter-nal, all things pen-e-trat-ing, for your rays our
4 Come, ce-les-tial Be-ing, make our hearts your dwell-ing, ev-'ry car-nal

God im-plor-ing. God is in the tem-ple; let all earth keep si-lence,
throne sur-round-ing! "Ho-ly, ho-ly, ho-ly!" Hear the hymn as-cend-ing,
soul is wait-ing. As the ten-der flow-ers, will-ing-ly un-fold-ing,
thought dis-pel-ling. By your Ho-ly Spir-it sanc-ti-fy us tru-ly,

bend-ing low in deep-est rev-'rence. You a-lone God we own,
songs of saints and an-gels blend-ing. Bow your ear to us here:
to the sun their fac-es hold-ing: e-ven so would we do,
teach-ing us to love you on-ly. Where we go here be-low,

Sov-'reign high, our Sav-ior; praise we sing for-ev-er!
hear, O Christ, the prais-es that your church now rais-es.
light from you ob-tain-ing, strength to serve you gain-ing.
let us bow be-fore you and in truth a-dore you.

Text: Gerhard Tersteegen, 1697–1769; tr . composite
Music: WUNDERBARER KÖNIG, Joachim Neander, 1650–1680

This revised version of a hymn of adoration from the early eighteenth century German Reformed church offers a more direct translation of the original "Gott ist gegenwärtig," one that addresses several language issues.—(Accompaniment: LBW 249)

God Loved the World

1 God loved the world so that he gave his on - ly
2 Christ Je - sus is the ground of faith, who was made
3 If you are ill, if death draws near, this truth your
4 Be of good cheer, for God's own Son for - gives all
5 All glo - ry to the Fa - ther, Son, and Ho - ly

Son the lost to save, that all who would in him be -
flesh and suf - fered death; all who con - fide in Christ a -
troub - led heart can cheer: Christ Je - sus saves your soul from
sins that you have done, and jus - ti - fied by Je - sus'
Spir - it, Three in One! To you, O bless - ed Trin - i -

lieve should ev - er - last - ing life re - ceive.
lone are built on this chief cor - ner - stone.
death; that is the firm - est ground of faith.
blood, your bap - tism grants the high - est good.
ty, be praise now and e - ter - nal - ly!

Text: *Gesangbuch*, Bollhagen, 1791; tr. August Crull, 1846–1923, alt.

Music: WALTON, W. Gardiner, *Sacred Melodies*, 1815

Here is a hymn text that is particularly useful during Lent, when John 3 occurs several times in the lectionary, with a tune that might encourage its wider use.

Hail the Day That Sees Him Rise

1 Hail the day that sees him rise, Al - le - lu - ia!
2 There the glo-rious tri - umph waits; Al - le - lu - ia!
3 See! he lifts his hands a - bove; Al - le - lu - ia!
4 Lord be-yond our mor - tal sight, Al - le - lu - ia!

glo - rious to his na - tive skies; Al - le - lu - ia!
lift your heads, e - ter - nal gates! Al - le - lu - ia!
See! he shows the prints of love: Al - le - lu - ia!
raise our hearts to reach thy height, Al - le - lu - ia!

Christ, a - while to mor - tals giv'n, Al - le - lu - ia!
Wide un - fold the ra - diant scene; Al - le - lu - ia!
Hark! his gra - cious lips be - stow, Al - le - lu - ia!
there thy face un - cloud - ed see, Al - le - lu - ia!

en - ters now the high - est heav'n! Al - le - lu - ia!
take the King of glo - ry in! Al - le - lu - ia!
bless-ings on his church be - low. Al - le - lu - ia!
find our heav'n of heav'ns in thee. Al - le - lu - ia!

Text: Charles Wesley, 1707–1788, alt.

Music: LLANFAIR, Robert Williams, c. 1781–1821

Appearing in *Service Book and Hymnal,* this Ascension hymn continues to appear in denominational worship books, most often to the tune also sung with "Christ the Lord is risen today; Alleluia!"—(Accompaniment: LBW 128)

Hark! A Thrilling Voice Is Sounding!

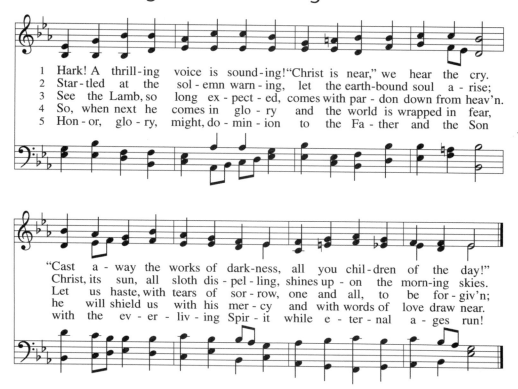

1 Hark! A thrill-ing voice is sound-ing! "Christ is near," we hear the cry.
2 Star-tled at the sol-emn warn-ing, let the earth-bound soul a - rise;
3 See the Lamb, so long ex-pect-ed, comes with par-don down from heav'n.
4 So, when next he comes in glo - ry and the world is wrapped in fear,
5 Hon - or, glo - ry, might, do-min - ion to the Fa - ther and the Son

"Cast a - way the works of dark-ness, all you chil-dren of the day!"
Christ, its sun, all sloth dis - pel - ling, shines up - on the morn-ing skies.
Let us haste, with tears of sor - row, one and all, to be for - giv'n;
he will shield us with his mer - cy and with words of love draw near.
with the ev - er - liv - ing Spir - it while e - ter - nal a - ges run!

Text: Latin hymn, 1632; tr. Edward Caswall, 1814–1878, alt.

Music: MERTON, William H. Monk, 1823–1889

Have Mercy on Us, Lord

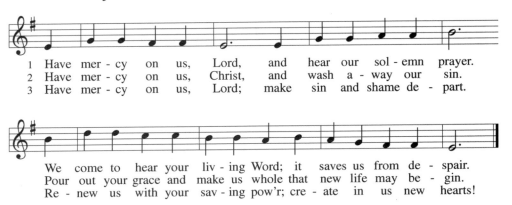

1 Have mer - cy on us, Lord, and hear our sol - emn prayer.
2 Have mer - cy on us, Christ, and wash a - way our sin.
3 Have mer - cy on us, Lord; make sin and shame de - part.

We come to hear your liv - ing Word; it saves us from de - spair.
Pour out your grace and make us whole that new life may be - gin.
Re - new us with your sav - ing pow'r; cre - ate in us new hearts!

Text: metrical Kyrie, Gracia Grindal, b. 1943

Music: SOUTHWELL, Daman, *Psalmes*, 1579

Text © 1998 Augsburg Fortress

Precedent for metrical paraphrases of liturgical texts reaches back before the Reformation to the medieval *leisen*. This text was part of a hymn mass commissioned for *Sundays and Seasons*. Paraphrases of the principal recurring portions of the eucharistic liturgy comprise the hymn mass texts, which can be sung to a variety of common tunes.—(Accompaniment: LBW 309)

Herald, Sound the Note of Judgment

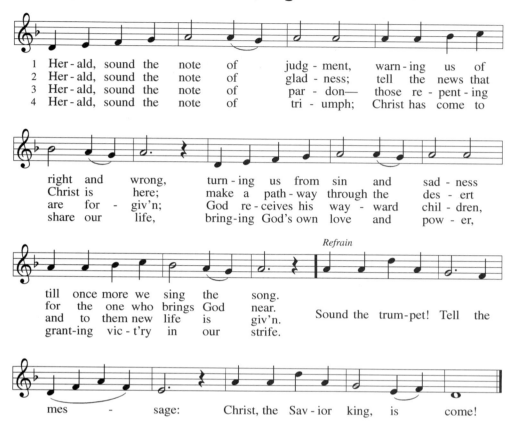

1 Her-ald, sound the note of judg-ment, warn-ing us of
2 Her-ald, sound the note of glad-ness; tell the news that
3 Her-ald, sound the note of par-don— those re-pent-ing
4 Her-ald, sound the note of tri-umph; Christ has come to

right and wrong, turn-ing us from sin and sad-ness
Christ is here; make a path-way through the des-ert
are for-giv'n; God re-ceives his way-ward chil-dren,
share our life, bring-ing God's own love and pow-er,

till once more we sing the song.
for the one who brings God near.
and to them new life is giv'n.   *Refrain* Sound the trum-pet! Tell the
grant-ing vic-t'ry in our strife.

mes - sage: Christ, the Sav-ior king, is come!

Text: Moir A. J. Waters, alt.

Music: PICARDY, French folk tune, 17th cent.

Text © Estate of Moir A. J. Waters, admin. Heather Bedford, 134 St. Lawrence Blvd, London ON N6J 2X1 Canada

Duplication in any form prohibited without permission or valid license from copyright administrator.

Introduced to Lutheran churches in *Lutheran Book of Worship*, this hymn marries well with the French folk tune PICARDY.
—(Accompaniment: LBW 198)

37

Holy, Holy, Lord Most Holy

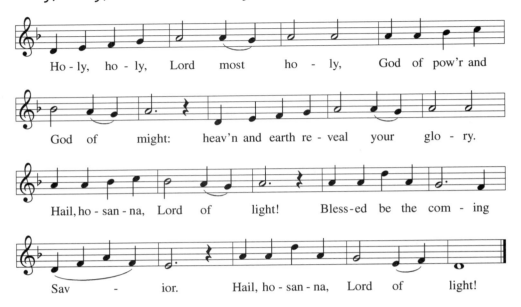

Ho-ly, ho-ly, Lord most ho-ly, God of pow'r and God of might: heav'n and earth re-veal your glo-ry. Hail, ho-san-na, Lord of light! Bless-ed be the com-ing Sav-ior. Hail, ho-san-na, Lord of light!

Text: metrical Sanctus, Martin A. Seltz, b. 1951

Music: PICARDY, French folk tune, 17th cent.

Text © 1998 Augsburg Fortress

Holy, Holy, Lord Most Holy

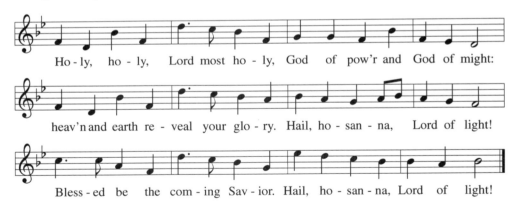

Ho-ly, ho-ly, Lord most ho-ly, God of pow'r and God of might: heav'n and earth re-veal your glo-ry. Hail, ho-san-na, Lord of light! Bless-ed be the com-ing Sav-ior. Hail, ho-san-na, Lord of light!

Text: metrical Sanctus, Martin A. Seltz, b. 1951

Music: REGENT SQUARE, Henry T. Smart, 1813–1879

Text © 1998 Augsburg Fortress

Precedent for metrical paraphrases of liturgical texts reaches back before the Reformation to the medieval *leisen*. This text was part of a hymn mass commissioned for *Sundays and Seasons.* Paraphrases of the principal recurring portions of the eucharistic liturgy comprise the hymn mass texts, which can be sung to a variety of common tunes.—(Accompaniment: LBW 198, LBW 50)

I Heard the Voice of Jesus Say

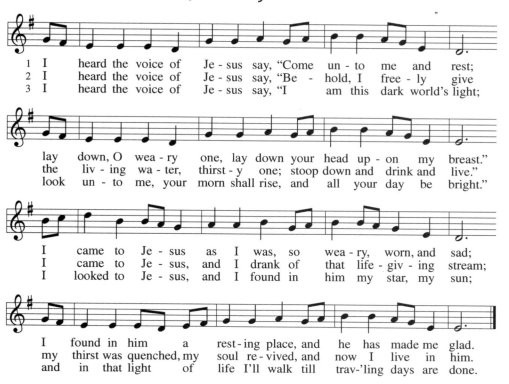

1 I heard the voice of Je - sus say, "Come un - to me and rest;
2 I heard the voice of Je - sus say, "Be - hold, I free - ly give
3 I heard the voice of Je - sus say, "I am this dark world's light;

lay down, O wea - ry one, lay down your head up - on my breast."
the liv - ing wa - ter, thirst - y one; stoop down and drink and live."
look un - to me, your morn shall rise, and all your day be bright."

I came to Je - sus as I was, so wea - ry, worn, and sad;
I came to Je - sus, and I drank of that life - giv - ing stream;
I looked to Je - sus, and I found in him my star, my sun;

I found in him a rest - ing place, and he has made me glad.
my thirst was quenched, my soul re - vived, and now I live in him.
and in that light of life I'll walk till trav - 'ling days are done.

Text: Horatius Bonar, 1808–1889
Music: KINGSFOLD, English melody

Rich in images from the gospels for Lent in lectionary year A, this hymn text is frequently combined with a folk melody from the British Isles, known in several versions as KINGSFOLD or STAR OF COUNTY DOWN.—(Accompaniment: WOV 730)

I Love to Tell the Story

1 I love to tell the sto - ry of un - seen things a - bove,
2 I love to tell the sto - ry: 'tis pleas - ant to re - peat
3 I love to tell the sto - ry, for those who know it best

of Je - sus and his glo - ry, of Je - sus and his love.
what seems, each time I tell it, more won - der - ful - ly sweet!
seem hun - ger - ing and thirst - ing to hear it like the rest.

I love to tell the sto - ry, be - cause I know it's true;
I love to tell the sto - ry, for some have nev - er heard
And when, in scenes of glo - ry, I sing the new, new song,

it sat - is - fies my long - ings as noth - ing else would do.
the mes - sage of sal - va - tion from God's own ho - ly word.
'twill be the old, old sto - ry that I have loved so long.

Refrain

I love to tell the sto - ry; 'twill be my theme in glo - ry

to tell the old, old sto - ry of Je - sus and his love.

Text: Katherine Hankey, 1834–1911
Music: HANKEY, William G. Fischer, 1835–1912

The words to certain hymns, especially those with refrains, are often deeply embedded in worshipers' memories. This version of a familiar gospel hymn preserves the original, slightly archaic language expressions.—(Accompaniment: LBW 390)

In Christ There Is No East or West

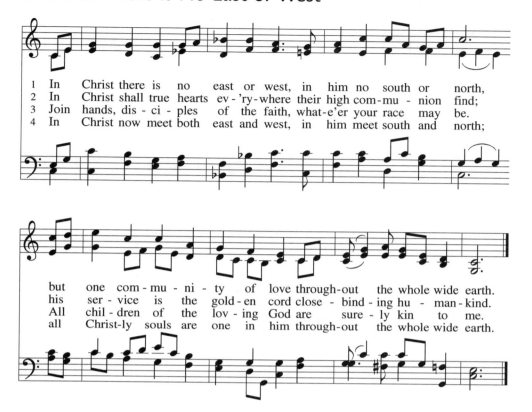

1 In Christ there is no east or west, in him no south or north,
2 In Christ shall true hearts ev-'ry-where their high com-mu - nion find;
3 Join hands, dis-ci - ples of the faith, what-e'er your race may be.
4 In Christ now meet both east and west, in him meet south and north;

but one com-mu - ni - ty of love through-out the whole wide earth.
his ser - vice is the gold - en cord close - bind - ing hu - man-kind.
All chil - dren of the lov - ing God are sure - ly kin to me.
all Christ-ly souls are one in him through-out the whole wide earth.

Text: John Oxenham, 1852–1941, alt.

Music: MCKEE, African American spiritual; adapt. Harry T. Burleigh, 1866–1949

John Oxenham's original text celebrating the unity of the human family has become less universal in its meaning as the English language has changed. This revised version restores the intent of the original.

In His Temple Now Behold Him

1 In his tem - ple now be - hold him, see the long - ex -
2 In the arms of her who bore him, vir - gin pure, be -
3 Je - sus, by your pre - sen - ta - tion, when they blessed you,
4 Prince and Au - thor of sal - va - tion, be your bound - less

pect - ed Lord; an - cient proph - ets had fore - told him,
hold him lie, while his a - ged saints a - dore him,
weak and poor, make us see your great sal - va - tion,
love our theme! Je - sus, praise to you be giv - en

God has now ful - filled his word. Now to praise him,
ere in per - fect faith they die. Al - le - lu - ia!
seal us with your prom - ise sure; and pre - sent us,
by the world you did re - deem, with the Fa - ther

his re - deem - ed shall break forth with one ac - cord.
Al - le - lu - ia! Lo, the in - car - nate God Most High!
in your glo - ry, to your Fa - ther, cleansed and pure.
and the Spir - it God of maj - es - ty su - preme!

Text: Henry J. Pye, 1825–1903, alt.

Music: WESTMINSTER ABBEY, Henry Purcell, 1659–1695; arr. Ernest Hawkins, 1802–1868

WESTMINSTER ABBEY is a widely used tune suitable for this hymn celebrating the presentation of Jesus in the temple. A doxological stanza has been restored.

In Peace and Joy I Now Depart

1 In peace and joy I now de - part as God is will - ing,
2 Christ Je - sus makes the way for me, my gra - cious Sav - ior;
3 The Lord is health and sav - ing light for ev - 'ry na - tion,

and faith fills all my mind and heart, calm - ing, still - ing.
with eyes of faith and trust I see God's great fa - vor.
dis - pel - ling shad - ows of the night with sal - va - tion:

God the Lord has prom-ised me that death is but a slum - ber.
When this life comes to an end, my hope is God's em - brac - ing.
Is - rael's praise and hope's de-light, my trea-sure, joy, and glo - ry.

Text: metrical Nunc dimittis, Martin Luther, 1483–1546, tr. composite

Music: MIT FRIED UND FREUD, Martin Luther, 1483–1546

Text © 2000 Augsburg Fortress

Precedent for metrical paraphrases of liturgical texts reaches back before the Reformation to the medieval *leisen*. This text is a translation of Luther's paraphrase of Luke 2:29-32, the song of Simeon in the temple.—(Accompaniment: LBW 349)

In the Bleak Midwinter

1 In the bleak mid - win - ter, frost - y wind made moan,
2 Heav - en can - not hold him, nor . . . . earth sus - tain;
3 An - gels and arch - an - gels may have gath - ered there,
4 What . . . can I give him, poor . . . . as I am?

earth stood hard as i - ron, wa - ter like a stone;
heaven and earth shall flee a - way when he comes to reign;
cher - u - bim and ser - a - phim throng - ed the air;
If I were a shep - herd I would bring a lamb;

snow had fall - en, snow on snow, snow on snow,
in the bleak mid - win - ter a sta - ble place suf - ficed
but his moth - er on - ly, in her maid - en bliss,
if I were a wise man I would do my part;

in the bleak mid - win - ter, long a - go.
the Lord . . . . God al - might - y, Je - sus Christ.
wor - shiped the Be - lov - ed with a kiss.
yet what I can I give him— give my heart.

Text: Christina Georgina Rossetti, 1830–1894
Music: CRANHAM, Gustav Theodore Holst, 1874–1934

44

In the Bleak Midwinter

1 In the bleak mid - win - ter, frost - y wind made moan,
2 Heav - en can - not hold him, nor .... earth sus - tain;
3 An - gels and arch - an - gels may have gath - ered there,
4 What ... can I give him, poor .... as I am?

earth stood hard as i - ron, wa - ter like a stone;
heav'n and earth shall flee a - way when he comes to reign;
cher - u - bim and ser - a - phim throng - ed the air;
If I were a shep - herd I would bring a lamb;

snow had fall - en, snow on snow, snow on snow,
in the bleak mid - win - ter a sta - ble place suf - ficed
but his moth - er on - ly, in her maid - en bliss,
if I were a wise man I would do my part;

in the bleak mid - win - ter, long a - go.
the Lord .... God al - might - y, Je - sus Christ.
wor - shiped the Be - lov - ed with a kiss.
yet what I can I give him— give my heart.

Text: Christina Georgina Rossetti, 1830–1894
Music: CRANHAM, Gustav Theodore Holst, 1874–1934

Appearing in *Service Book and Hymnal* and continuing to appear in numerous other worship books, this hymn remains a favorite for Christmas and Epiphany.

Lift Every Voice and Sing

1 Lift ev-'ry voice and sing till earth and heav-en ring,
2 Ston-y the road we trod, bit-ter the chas-t'ning rod,
3 God of our wea-ry years, God of our si-lent tears,

ring with the har-mo-nies of lib-er-ty.
felt in the days when hope un-born had died;
thou who hast brought us thus far on the way;

Let our re-joic-ing rise high as the lis-t'ning skies,
yet with a stead-y beat, have not our wea-ry feet
thou who hast by thy might led us in-to the light,

let it re-sound loud as the roll-ing sea.
come to the place for which our par-ents sighed?
keep us for-ev-er in the path, we pray.

Sing a song full of the faith that the dark past has taught us;
We have come o-ver a way that with tears has been wa-tered;
Lest our feet stray from the plac-es, our God, where we met thee;

sing a song full of the hope that the pres-ent has brought us;
we have come, tread-ing our path through the blood of the slaugh - tered,
lest, our hearts drunk with the wine of the world, we for-get thee;

fac-ing the ris-ing sun of our new day be - gun,
out from the gloom-y past, till now we stand at last
shad-owed be-neath thy hand, may we for-ev-er stand,

let us march on till vic-to - ry is won.
where the white gleam of our bright star is cast.
true to our God, true to our na - tive land.

Text: James Weldon Johnson, 1871–1938
Music: LIFT EVERY VOICE, J. Rosamond Johnson, 1873–1954

From the time of its introduction in 1900, this song rapidly gained acceptance and today is considered by many African Americans to be a national anthem. This version restores a singable harmony closely based on the original.

Lift Up Your Heads, Ye Mighty Gates

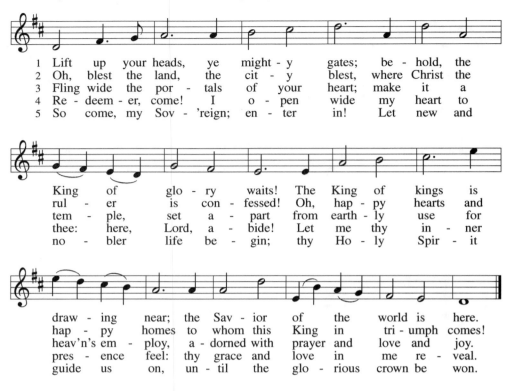

1 Lift up your heads, ye might-y gates; be-hold, the
2 Oh, blest the land, the cit-y blest, where Christ the
3 Fling wide the por-tals of your heart; make it a
4 Re-deem-er, come! I o-pen wide my heart to
5 So come, my Sov-'reign; en-ter in! Let new and

King of glo-ry waits! The King of kings is
rul-er is con-fessed! Oh, hap-py hearts and
tem-ple, set a-part from earth-ly use for
thee: here, Lord, a-bide! Let me thy in-ner
no-bler life be-gin; thy Ho-ly Spir-it

draw-ing near; the Sav-ior of the world is here.
hap-py homes to whom this King in tri-umph comes!
heav'n's em-ploy, a-dorned with prayer and love and joy.
pres-ence feel: thy grace and love in me re-veal.
guide us on, un-til the glo-rious crown be won.

Text: Georg Weissel, 1590–1635; tr. Catherine Winkworth, 1829–1878
Music: TRURO, T. Williams, *Psalmodia Evangelica*, 1789

Based on Psalm 24:7-9, this hymn is presented with a translation and tune that has broad ecumenical acceptance in addition to its use in *Service Book and Hymnal*.—(Accompaniment: LBW 363)

Lo, How a Rose E'er Blooming

1 Lo, how a rose e'er bloom-ing from ten - der stem hath sprung!
2 I - sai - ah 'twas fore - told it, the rose I have in mind;
3 This flow'r, whose fra-grance ten - der with sweet-ness fills the air,
4 O Sav - ior, child of Mar - y, who felt our hu - man woe;

Of Jes - se's lin - eage com - ing as proph-ets long have sung,
with Mar - y we be - hold it, the vir - gin moth - er kind.
dis - pels with glo - rious splen - dor the dark-ness ev - 'ry - where.
O Sav - ior, king of glo - ry, who dost our weak - ness know:

it came, a flow'r - et bright, a - mid the cold of
To show God's love a - right, she bore to us a
True man, yet ver - y God, from sin and death he
bring us at length we pray to the bright courts of

win - ter, when half - spent was the night.
Sav - ior, when half - spent was the night.
saves us and light - ens ev - 'ry load.
heav - en, and to the end - less day.

Text: German, 15th cent.; tr. Theodore Baker, 1851–1934, sts. 1–2; Harriet R. Krauth, 1845–1925, st. 3; John Caspar
Mattes, 1876–1948, st. 4

Music: Es ist ein Ros, *Alte Catholische Geistliche Kirchengesäng,* Köln, 1599

Isaiah 11:1-10 is the primary source for the image that unfolds in this carol, included here with a commonly used
translation that appeared in *Service Book and Hymnal.*—(Accompaniment: LBW 58)

My Shepherd, You Supply My Need

1 My Shepherd, you supply my need; most holy is your name. In pastures fresh you make me feed, beside the living stream. You bring my wand'ring spirit back when I forsake your ways, and lead me, for your mercy's sake, in paths of truth and grace.

2 When I walk through the shades of death, your presence is my stay; one word of your supporting breath drives all my fears away. Your hand, in sight of all my foes, does still my table spread; my cup with blessings overflows, your oil anoints my head.

3 The sure provisions of my God attend me all my days; oh, may your house be my abode and all my work be praise. There would I find a settled rest, while others go and come; no more a stranger or a guest, but like a child at home.

Text: Psalm 23, para. Isaac Watts, 1674–1748, alt.
Music: RESIGNATION, North American folk melody

My Shepherd, You Supply My Need

1 My Shep-herd, you sup-ply my need, most ho-ly is your
2 When I walk through the shades of death, your pres-ence is my
3 The sure pro-vi-sions of my God at-tend me all my

name. In pas-tures fresh you make me feed, be-side the
stay; one word of your sup-port-ing breath drives all my
days; oh, may your house be my a-bode and all my

liv-ing stream. You bring my wan-d'ring spir-it
fears a-way. Your hand, in sight of all my
work be praise. There would I find a set-tled

back when I for-sake your ways, and lead me, for your
foes, does still my ta-ble spread; my cup with bless-ings
rest, while oth-ers go and come; no more a strang-er

mer-cy's sake, in paths of truth and grace.
o-ver-flows, your oil a-noints my head.
or a guest, but like a child at home.

Text: Psalm 23, para. Isaac Watts, 1674–1748, alt.
Music: RESIGNATION, North American folk melody

Although Isaac Watts's paraphrase of Psalm 23 has been sung with this shape-note melody since the middle of the nineteenth century, only in the last several decades has it begun to appear in major denominational worship books. The text is placed in the second person in this version.

O Blessed Spring

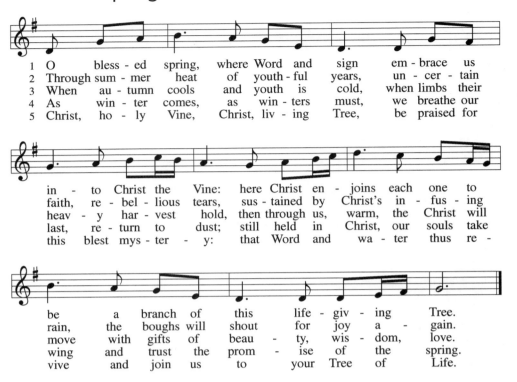

1 O bless-ed spring, where Word and sign em-brace us
2 Through sum-mer heat of youth-ful years, un-cer-tain
3 When au-tumn cools and youth is cold, when limbs their
4 As win-ter comes, as win-ters must, we breathe our
5 Christ, ho-ly Vine, Christ, liv-ing Tree, be praised for

in-to Christ the Vine: here Christ en-joins each one to
faith, re-bel-lious tears, sus-tained by Christ's in-fus-ing
heav-y har-vest hold, then through us, warm, the Christ will
last, re-turn to dust; still held in Christ, our souls take
this blest mys-ter-y: that Word and wa-ter thus re-

be a branch of this life-giv-ing Tree.
rain, the boughs will shout for joy a-gain.
move with gifts of beau-ty, wis-dom, love.
wing and trust the prom-ise of the spring.
vive and join us to your Tree of Life.

Text: Susan Palo Cherwien, b. 1953

Music: O WALY WALY, English tune

Text © 1993 Susan Palo Cherwien, admin. Augsburg Fortress

Though less than a decade old, this hymn celebrating baptism and the seasons of the Christian life has already received significant ecumenical attention. In addition to the tune BERGLUND that appears in *With One Voice,* the text has also been published with this English melody sometimes associated with the folk song "The Water Is Wide."—(Accompaniment: WOV 749)

O Lamb of God, You Bear the Sin

1 O Lamb of God, you bear the sin of all the world a - way;
2 O Lamb of God, you bear the sin of all the world a - way;
3 O Lamb of God, you bear the sin of all the world a - way;

you suf - fered death our lives to save: have mer - cy now, we pray.
you set us free from guilt and grave: have mer - cy now, we pray.
e - ter - nal peace with God you made: give us your peace, we pray.

Text: metrical Agnus Dei, Martin A. Seltz, b. 1951

Music: LAND OF REST, North American

Text © 1998 Augsburg Fortress

Precedent for metrical paraphrases of liturgical texts reaches back before the Reformation to the medieval *leisen.* This text was part of a hymn mass commissioned for *Sundays and Seasons.* Paraphrases of the principal recurring portions of the eucharistic liturgy comprise the hymn mass texts, which can be sung to a variety of common tunes.—(Accompaniment: LBW 331)

O Sacred Head, Now Wounded

1 O sa - cred head, now wound - ed, with grief and shame weighed down,
2 How art thou pale with an - guish, with sore a - buse and scorn;
3 What lan - guage shall I bor - row to thank thee, dear - est friend,
4 Lord, be my con - so - la - tion; shield me when I must die;

now scorn - ful - ly sur - round - ed with thorns, thine on - ly crown;
how does that vis - age lan - guish which once was bright as morn!
for this thy dy - ing sor - row, thy pit - y with - out end?
re - mind me of thy pas - sion when my last hour draws nigh.

O sa - cred head, what glo - ry, what bliss till now was thine!
Thy grief and bit - ter pas - sion were all for sin - ners' gain;
Oh, make me thine for - ev - er, and should I faint-ing be,
These eyes, new faith re - ceiv - ing, from thee shall nev - er move;

Yet, though de - spised and gor - y, I joy to call thee mine.
mine, mine was the trans - gres - sion, but thine the dead - ly pain.
Lord, let me nev - er, nev - er out - live my love to thee.
for they who die be - liev - ing die safe - ly in thy love.

Text: Paul Gerhardt, 1607–1676, based on Arnulf of Louvain, c. 1250; tr. composite

Music: HERZLICH TUT MICH VERLANGEN, German melody, c. 1500, adapt. Hans L. Hassler, 1564–1612; arr. J. S. Bach, 1685–1750

This hymn, based on a medieval meditation on the death of Christ, is often sung in a harmonization by J. S. Bach. The *St. Matthew Passion* is the source for the harmonization presented here.

O Come, O Come, Emmanuel

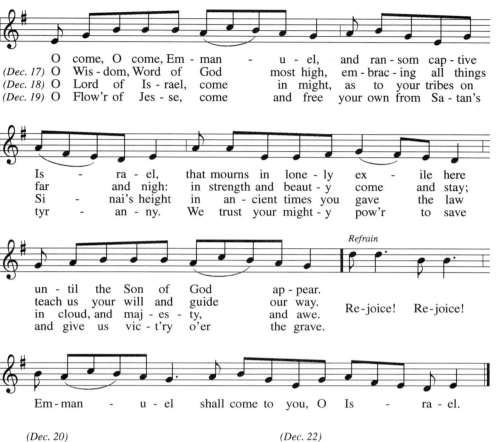

O come, O come, Em - man - u - el, and ran - som cap - tive
(Dec. 17) O Wis - dom, Word of God most high, em - brac - ing all things
(Dec. 18) O Lord of Is - rael, come in might, as to your tribes on
(Dec. 19) O Flow'r of Jes - se, come and free your own from Sa - tan's

Is - ra - el, that mourns in lone - ly ex - ile here
far and nigh: in strength and beaut - y come and stay;
Si - nai's height in an - cient times you gave the law
tyr - an - ny. We trust your might - y pow'r to save

Refrain

un - til the Son of God ap - pear.
teach us your will and guide our way.
in cloud, and maj - es - ty, and awe. Re - joice! Re - joice!
and give us vic - t'ry o'er the grave.

Em - man - u - el shall come to you, O Is - ra - el.

(Dec. 20)
O Key of David, Holy One,
come, open wide our heav'nly home;
make safe the way that leads on high,
and close the path to misery. *Refrain*

(Dec. 21)
O Dayspring, come with light and cheer;
O Sun of justice, now draw near.
Disperse the gloomy clouds of night,
and death's dark shadow put to flight. *Refrain*

(Dec. 22)
O Ruler of the nations, come,
O Cornerstone that binds in one:
refresh the hearts that long for you;
restore the broken, make us new. *Refrain*

(Dec. 23)
O come, O come, Emmanuel,
and ransom captive Israel,
that mourns in lonely exile here
until the Son of God appear. *Refrain*

Text: *Psalteriolum Cantionum Catholicarum*, Köln, 1710; tr. composite

Music: VENI EMMANUEL, French processional, 15th cent.

Text © 1997 Augsburg Fortress

The O antiphons upon which this hymn is based have traditionally been sung at evening prayer from December 17 through 23, one antiphon each day. The appointed dates are included in this complete version of the hymn, although any and all of the stanzas may be sung at any time during Advent. The translation is an adaptation and expansion of one prepared by John M. Neale in the nineteenth century.—(Accompaniment: LBW 34)

Oh, What Shall I Render

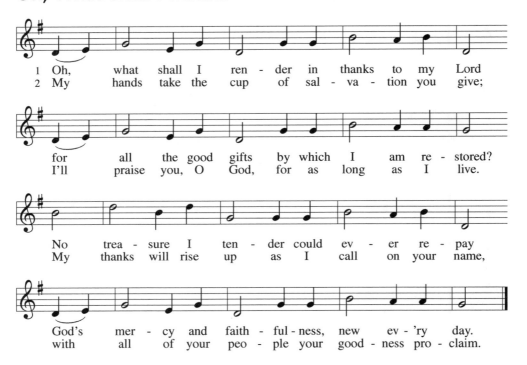

1 Oh, what shall I ren - der in thanks to my Lord
2 My hands take the cup of sal - va - tion you give;

for all the good gifts by which I am re - stored?
I'll praise you, O God, for as long as I live.

No trea - sure I ten - der could ev - er re - pay
My thanks will rise up as I call on your name,

God's mer - cy and faith - ful - ness, new ev - 'ry day.
with all of your peo - ple your good - ness pro - claim.

Text: metrical offertory canticle based on Psalm 116, Martin A. Seltz, b. 1951

Music: FOUNDATION, early North American

Text © 1998 Augsburg Fortress

Precedent for metrical paraphrases of liturgical texts reaches back before the Reformation to the medieval *leisen*. This text was part of a hymn mass commissioned for *Sundays and Seasons*. Paraphrases of the principal recurring portions of the eucharistic liturgy comprise the hymn mass texts, which can be sung to a variety of common tunes.—(Accompaniment: LBW 507)

Praise and Thanks and Adoration

1 Praise and thanks and ad-o-ra-tion, Son of God, to you we give,
2 Hold me ev-er in your keep-ing, com-fort me in pain and strife;

for you chose to serve cre-a-tion, died that Ad-am's heirs might live.
through my laugh-ter and my weep-ing, lift me to a no-bler life.

Dear Lord Je-sus, guide my way; faith-ful let me day by day
Draw my fer-vent love to you; con-stant hope and faith re-new

fol-low where your steps are lead-ing, find ad-ven-ture, joys ex-ceed-ing!
in your birth, your life and pas-sion, in your death and res-ur-rec-tion.

Text: Thomas H. Kingo, 1634–1703; tr. *Lutheran Book of Worship,* 1978

Music: FREU DICH SEHR, *Trente quatre pseaumes de David,* Geneva, 1551

Text © 1978 *Lutheran Book of Worship,* admin. Augsburg Fortress

This text and tune are paired in *Lutheran Book of Worship,* but here the tune is given in its rhythmic version. A sprightly Renaissance dance captures well the spirit of this form of the tune.—(Accompaniment: LBW 29)

Praise to the Lord, the Almighty

1 Praise to the Lord, the Al - might - y, the God of cre -
2 Praise the Al - might - y, o'er all life so won - drous - ly
3 Praise the Al - might - y, who pros - pers your work and de -
4 Praise the Al - might - y! In won - der my spir - it is

a - tion! My heart is long - ing to of - fer up sweet ad - o -
reign - ing, and, as on wings of an ea - gle, up - lift - ing, sus -
fends you; see from the heav - ens the show - ers of mer - cy God
soar - ing! All that has life and breath, come now with prais - es out -

ra - tion. Mel - o - dy make; dul - ci - mer, harp, now a -
tain - ing. Have you not seen? All that is need - ful has
sends you. Pon - der a - new what the Al - might - y can
pour - ing. Let the a - men sound from God's peo - ple a -

wake. Sound forth your praise, ev - 'ry na - tion.
been sent by God's gra - cious or - dain - ing.
do; in - fi - nite Love here be - friends you.
gain, glad - ly for - ev - er a - dor - ing!

Text: Joachim Neander, 1650–1680; tr. composite

Music: LOBE DEN HERREN, *Ernewerten Gesangbuch*, Stralsund, 1655

Text © 2000 Augsburg Fortress

This is the best known of the hymns of Joachim Neander, a pastor of the Reformed church in Düsseldorf, Germany. This version attempts to address a number of language issues while retaining much of Catherine Winkworth's familiar translation. See "Sing Praise to God" in this collection for another approach to this text, one that uses a new translation.— (Accompaniment: LBW 543)

Praise, My Soul, the God of Heaven

1 Praise, my soul, the God of heav-en; joy-ful-ly your trib-ute bring.
2 God be praised for grace and fa-vor to our fore-bears in dis-tress.
3 Frail as sum-mer's flow'r we flour-ish, blows the wind and it is gone;
4 An-gels sing in ad-o-ra-tion, in God's pres-ence, face to face.

Ran-somed, healed, re-stored, for-giv-en, ev-er-more God's prais-es sing.
God be praised, the same for-ev-er, slow to chide and swift to bless.
but, as mor-tals rise and per-ish, God en-dures un-chang-ing on.
Sun and moon and all cre-a-tion, all who dwell in time and space:

Al-le-lu-ia! Al-le-lu-ia! Prais-es ev-er-last-ing ring!
Al-le-lu-ia! Al-le-lu-ia! Glo-rious is God's faith-ful-ness!
Al-le-lu-ia! Al-le-lu-ia! Praise the great E-ter-nal One!
Al-le-lu-ia! Al-le-lu-ia! Praise with us the God of grace.

Text: Henry F. Lyte, 1793–1847, adapt. composite
Music: PRAISE, MY SOUL, John Goss, 1800–1880

Portions of Psalm 103 are paraphrased in this hymn text, which has been adapted from Henry Lyte's original to provide a greater balance of images for God.—(Accompaniment: LBW 549)

Restore in Us, O God

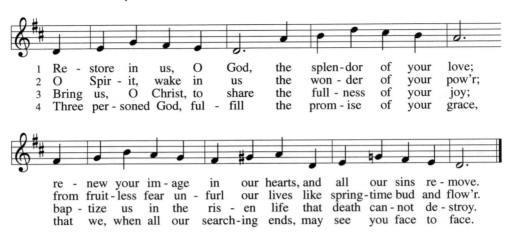

1 Re - store in us, O God, the splen-dor of your love;
2 O Spir - it, wake in us the won - der of your pow'r;
3 Bring us, O Christ, to share the full - ness of your joy;
4 Three per - soned God, ful - fill the prom - ise of your grace,

re - new your im - age in our hearts, and all our sins re - move.
from fruit - less fear un - furl our lives like spring - time bud and flow'r.
bap - tize us in the ris - en life that death can - not de - stroy.
that we, when all our search - ing ends, may see you face to face.

Text: Carl P. Daw Jr., b. 1944

Music: POTSDAM , Mercer, *Church Psalter,* 1854

Carl Daw's hymn, with its themes of baptism and renewal, is a much needed addition to the repertoire especially during the season of Lent, which has recently seen a revival of these themes. Two common tunes are offered here to supplement the new tune that was published in *With One Voice.*—(Accompaniment: LBW 89)

Restore in Us, O God

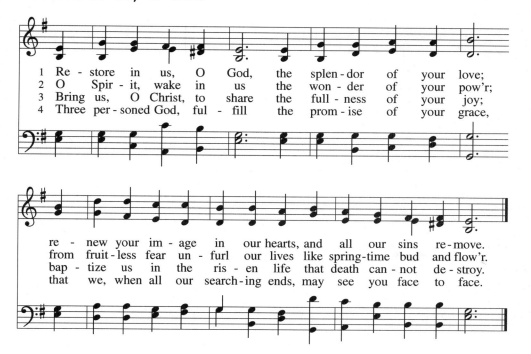

1 Re - store in us, O God, the splen - dor of your love;
2 O Spir - it, wake in us the won - der of your pow'r;
3 Bring us, O Christ, to share the full - ness of your joy;
4 Three per - soned God, ful - fill the prom - ise of your grace,

re - new your im - age in our hearts, and all our sins re - move.
from fruit - less fear un - furl our lives like spring-time bud and flow'r.
bap - tize us in the ris - en life that death can - not de - stroy.
that we, when all our search - ing ends, may see you face to face.

Text: Carl P. Daw Jr. b. 1944

Music: SOUTHWELL, Daman, *Psalmes,* 1579

Carl Daw's hymn, with its themes of baptism and renewal, is a much needed addition to the repertoire especially during the season of Lent, which has recently seen a revival of these themes. Two common tunes are offered here to supplement the new tune that was published in *With One Voice.*

Ride On, Ride On in Majesty

1 Ride on, ride on in maj - es-ty! Hear all the tribes ho - san - na cry;
2 Ride on, ride on in maj - es-ty! In low - ly pomp ride on to die.
3 Ride on, ride on in maj - es-ty! The wing-ed squad-rons of the sky
4 Ride on, ride on in maj - es-ty! Your last and fierc - est strife is nigh.
5 Ride on, ride on in maj - es-ty! In low - ly pomp ride on to die,

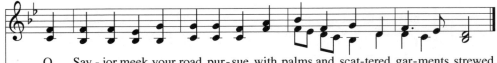

O Sav - ior meek, your road pur-sue, with palms and scat-tered gar-ments strewed.
O Christ, your tri-umphs now be - gin o'er cap - tive death and con-quered sin.
look down with sad and won-d'ring eyes to see the ap-proach-ing sac - ri - fice.
The Fa - ther on his sap-phire throne a - waits his own a - noint - ed Son.
bow your meek head to mor-tal pain, then take, O Christ, your pow'r and reign!

Text: Henry H. Milman, 1791–1868, alt.
Music: St. Drostane, John B. Dykes, 1823–1876

St. Drostane is a tune familiar to many Lutherans from its use in *Service Book and Hymnal*. Its steady pace is fitting for a hymn often sung unaccompanied in procession on Palm Sunday.

Rise, O Church, like Christ Arisen

1 Rise, O church, like Christ a - ris - en, from this meal of love and grace;
2 Rise, trans-formed, and choose to fol - low af - ter Christ, though wound-ed, whole;
3 Rise, re - mem - ber well the fu - ture God has called us to re - ceive;
4 Ser - vice be our sure vo - ca - tion; cour-age be our dai - ly breath;

may we through such love en - vi - sion whose we are, and whose, our praise.
bro - ken, shared, our lives are hal - lowed to re - lease and to con - sole.
pres - ent by God's lov - ing nur - ture, spir - it - ed then let us live.
mer - cy be our des - ti - na - tion from this day and un - to death.

Al - le - lu - ia, al - le - lu - ia: God, the won - der of our days.
Al - le - lu - ia, al - le - lu - ia: Christ, our pres - ent, past, and goal.
Al - le - lu - ia, al - le - lu - ia: Spir - it, grace by whom we live.
Al - le - lu - ia, al - le - lu - ia: Rise, O church, a liv - ing faith.

Text: Susan Palo Cherwien, b. 1953

Music: PRAISE, MY SOUL, John Goss, 1800–1880

Text © 1997 Susan Palo Cherwien, admin. Augsburg Fortress

John Goss's best known tune (see "Praise, my soul, the God of heaven" in this collection) is given additional life through its pairing with this newer text celebrating the resurrection of Christ in the church of Christ.—(Accompaniment: LBW 549)

Savior, like a Shepherd Lead Us

1 Sav-ior like a shep-herd lead us; much we need your ten-der care.
2 We are yours; in love be-friend us, be the guard-ian of our way;
3 You have prom-ised to re-ceive us, poor and sin-ful though we be;
4 Ear-ly let us seek your fa-vor, ear-ly let us do your will;

In your pleas-ant pas-tures feed us, for our use your fold pre-pare.
keep your flock, from sin de-fend us, seek us when we go a-stray.
you have mer-cy to re-lieve us, grace to cleanse, and pow'r to free.
bless-ed Lord and on-ly Sav-ior, with your love our spir-its fill.

Bless-ed Je-sus, bless-ed Je-sus, you have bought us; we are yours.
Bless-ed Je-sus, bless-ed Je-sus, hear us chil-dren when we pray.
Bless-ed Je-sus, bless-ed Je-sus, ear-ly let us turn to you.
Bless-ed Je-sus, bless-ed Je-sus, you have loved us, love us still.

Bless-ed Je-sus, bless-ed Je-sus, you have bought us; we are yours.
Bless-ed Je-sus, bless-ed Je-sus, hear us chil-dren when we pray.
Bless-ed Je-sus, bless-ed Je-sus, ear-ly let us turn to you.
Bless-ed Je-sus, bless-ed Je-sus, you have loved us, love us still.

Text: attr. Dorothy A. Thrupp, 1779–1847
Music: BRADBURY, William B. Bradbury, 1816–1868

64   William Bradbury's tune is often associated with this hymn text evoking the image of Jesus, the good shepherd. The text first appeared anonymously in *Hymns for the Young* (c. 1836), edited by Dorothy Ann Thrupp.

Savior of the Nations, Come

1 Sav - ior of the na - tions, come; vir-gin's son, make here your home.
2 Not by hu - man flesh and blood, by the Spir - it of our God
3 Won-drous birth! Oh, won-drous child of the vir - gin un - de - filed!
4 God the Fa - ther is his source, back to God he runs his course;

Mar - vel now, O heav'n and earth, that the Lord chose such a birth.
was the Word of God made flesh, wom-an's off - spring, pure and fresh.
Might-y God and man in one, ea - ger now his race to run!
down to death and hell de - scends, God's high throne he re - as - cends.

5 Come, O ageless Father's Peer;
gird your might in mortal gear.
Take on flesh to rout the wrong,
make our flesh in frailty strong.

6 Now your manger's halo bright
hallows night with newborn light;
let no night this light subdue,
let our faith shine ever new.

7 Praise to God the Father sing,
praise to God the Son, our king,
praise to God the Spirit be
ever and eternally.

Text: attr. Ambrose of Milan, 340–397; tr. William M. Reynolds, 1816–1876, and Martin L. Seltz, 1909–1967

Music: NUN KOMM, DER HEIDEN HEILAND, J. Walter, *Geistliche Gesangbüchlein,* 1524

Text sts. 3–6 © 1969 Concordia Publishing House, 3558 S. Jefferson Ave., St. Louis MO 63118, (800) 325-0191.

This version of an ancient Advent hymn, ascribed to St. Ambrose by his contemporary and disciple St. Augustine, first appeared in *Worship Supplement* (1969). The translation follows the meter of the German version prepared by Martin Luther in 1523.—(Accompaniment: LBW 28)

Sing, My Tongue

1 Sing, my tongue, the glo - rious bat - tle; sing the end - ing
2 Tell how, when at length the full - ness of the ap - point - ed
3 Thus, with thir - ty years ac - com - plished, he went forth from
4 Faith - ful cross, true sign of tri - umph, be for all the
5 Un - to God be praise and glo - ry; to the Fa - ther

of the fray. Now a - bove the cross, the troph - y,
time was come, he, the Word, was born of wom - an,
Naz - a - reth, des - tined, ded - i - cat - ed, will - ing,
no - blest tree; none in fo - liage, none in blos - som,
and the Son, to the e - ter - nal Spir - it hon - or

sound the loud tri - um - phant lay; tell how Christ, the world's re -
left for us his Fa - ther's home, blazed the path of true o -
did his work, and met his death; like a lamb he hum - bly
none in fruit your e - qual be; sym - bol of the world's re -
now and ev - er - more be done; praise and glo - ry in the

deem - er, as a vic - tim won the day.
be - dience, shone as light a - midst the gloom.
yield - ed on the cross his dy - ing breath.
demp - tion, for your bur - den makes us free.
high - est, while the time - less a - ges run.

Text: Venantius Honorius Fortunatus, 530–609; tr. John M. Neale, 1818–1866, alt.

Music: PICARDY, French folk tune, 17th cent.

Another frequent text and tune marriage in ecumenical circles is this ancient hymn honoring the holy cross, set to a folk tune named for a province in northern France.—(Accompaniment: LBW 198)

Sing Praise to God, Who Has Shaped

1 Sing praise to God, who has shaped and sus-tains all cre-
2 Praise God, our guard-ian, who lov-ing-ly of-fers cor-
3 Sing praise to God, with sin-cere thanks for all your suc-
4 Sing praise, my soul, the great name of your high God com-

a - tion! Sing praise, my soul, in pro-found and com-plete ad-o-
rec - tion, who, as on ea-gle's wings, saves us from sin-ful de-
cess - es. Mer-ci-ful God ev-er loves to en-cour-age and
mend - ing. All that have life and breath join you, their notes sweet-ly

ra - tion! Glad-some re-joice, or-gan and trum-pet and
jec - tion. Have you ob-served, how we are al-ways pre-
bless us. On-ly con-ceive what god-ly strength can a-
blend - ing. God is your light! Soul, ev-er keep this in

voice, join-ing God's great con-gre-ga-tion.
served by God's pa-ren-tal af-fec-tion?
chieve: strength that would touch and car-ess us.
sight. A-men, a-men nev-er end-ing.

Text: Joachim Neander, 1650–1680; tr. Madeleine Forell Marshall, b. 1946
Music: LOBE DEN HERREN, *Ernewerten Gesangbuch*, Stralsund, 1655
Text © 1993 Madeleine Forell Marshall, admin. Augsburg Fortress

This is the best known of the hymns of Joachim Neander, a pastor of the Reformed church in Düsseldorf, Germany. This version attempts to address a number of language issues by means of a new translation. See "Praise to the Lord, the Almighty" in this collection for another approach to this text, one that retains much of Catherine Winkworth's familiar translation.—(Accompaniment: LBW 543)

Sing with All the Saints in Glory

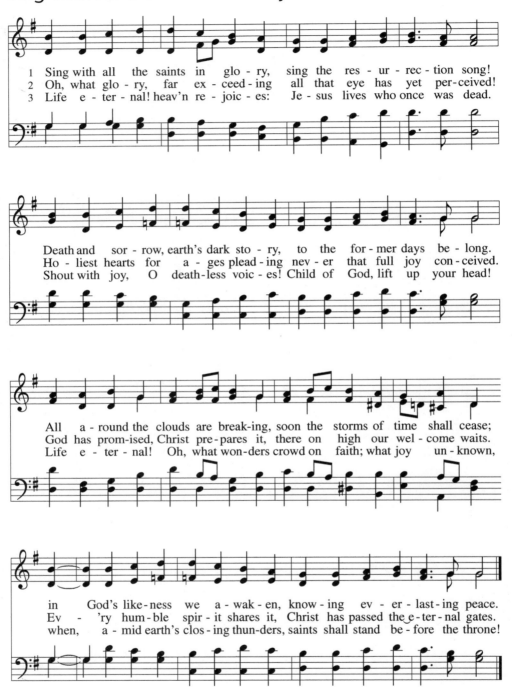

1 Sing with all the saints in glo - ry, sing the res - ur - rec - tion song!
2 Oh, what glo - ry, far ex - ceed - ing all that eye has yet per-ceived!
3 Life e - ter - nal! heav'n re - joic - es: Je - sus lives who once was dead.

Death and sor - row, earth's dark sto - ry, to the for - mer days be - long.
Ho - liest hearts for a - ges plead - ing nev - er that full joy con - ceived.
Shout with joy, O death-less voic - es! Child of God, lift up your head!

All a - round the clouds are break-ing, soon the storms of time shall cease;
God has prom-ised, Christ pre-pares it, there on high our wel - come waits.
Life e - ter - nal! Oh, what won-ders crowd on faith; what joy un - known,

in God's like - ness we a - wak - en, know - ing ev - er - last-ing peace.
Ev - 'ry hum - ble spir - it shares it, Christ has passed the e - ter - nal gates.
when, a - mid earth's clos - ing thun-ders, saints shall stand be - fore the throne!

Text: William J. Irons, 1812–1883, alt.

Music: HYMN TO JOY, Ludwig van Beethoven, 1770–1827, adapt.

68

In addition to the newer tune available in *With One Voice* (no. 691), this text by William Irons is often paired with a tune derived from Beethoven's Ninth Symphony. Here Beethoven's tune is given in its original rhythmic form.

Strengthen for Service, Lord

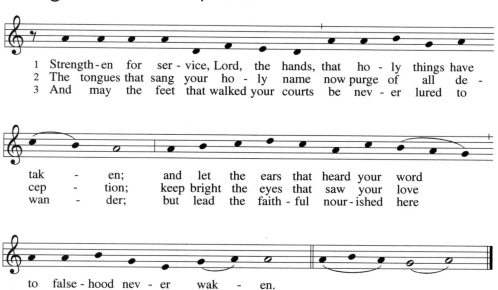

1 Strength-en for ser - vice, Lord, the hands, that ho - ly things have
2 The tongues that sang your ho - ly name now purge of all de -
3 And may the feet that walked your courts be nev - er lured to

tak - en; and let the ears that heard your word
cep - tion; keep bright the eyes that saw your love
wan - der; but lead the faith - ful nour - ished here

to false - hood nev - er wak - en.
and shar - pen their per - cep - tion.
to jour - ney on in splen - dor. A - men

Text: Syriac Liturgy of Malabar; tr. *The English Hymnal*, 1906, adapt.
Music: JESU DULCIS MEMORIA, plainsong, mode 1

Ephraim the Syrian, who lived in Northern Mesopotamia in the fourth century, is believed by some to be the author of the prayer from which this hymn is derived. The prayer is a part of the communion rite in the Liturgy of Malabar, which survives today in the Nestorian rite used in South India. Here it is set to a plainsong tune.—(Accompaniment: WOV 659)

Thank the Lord, Your Voices Raise

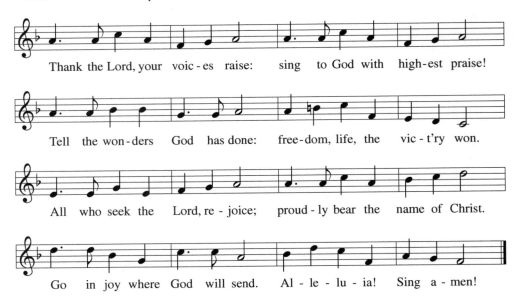

Thank the Lord, your voic-es raise: sing to God with high-est praise!

Tell the won-ders God has done: free-dom, life, the vic-t'ry won.

All who seek the Lord, re - joice; proud - ly bear the name of Christ.

Go in joy where God will send. Al - le - lu - ia! Sing a - men!

Text: metrical post-communion canticle, Martin A. Seltz, b. 1951

Music: St. George's Windsor, George J. Elvey, 1816–1893

Text © 1998 Augsburg Fortress

Precedent for metrical paraphrases of liturgical texts reaches back before the Reformation to the medieval *leisen.* This text was part of a hymn mass commissioned for *Sundays and Seasons.* Paraphrases of the principal recurring portions of the eucharistic liturgy comprise the hymn mass texts, which can be sung to a variety of common tunes.—(Accompaniment: LBW 407)

That Easter Day with Joy Was Bright

1 That Eas - ter day with joy was bright; the sun shone
2 O Je - sus, king of gen - tle - ness, with con - stant
3 O Christ, you are the Lord of all in this our
4 All praise, O ris - en Lord, we give to you, once

out with fair - er light, when, to their long - ing
love our hearts pos - sess; to you our lips will
Eas - ter fes - ti - val, for you will be our
dead, but now a - live! To God the Fa - ther

eyes re - stored, the a - pos - tles saw their ris - en Lord!
ev - er raise the trib - ute of our grate - ful praise.
strength and shield from ev - 'ry weap - on death can wield.
e - qual praise, and God the Ho - ly Ghost, we raise!

Text: Latin hymn, 4th or 5th cent.; tr. John M. Neale, 1818–1866, alt.
Music: PUER NOBIS, adapt. Michael Praetorius, 1571–1621

PUER NOBIS is a tune often associated with this ancient Easter hymn, sung for centuries as a morning hymn each day from the Sunday after Easter until Ascension.—(Accompaniment: LBW 36)

That Easter Day with Joy Was Bright

1 That Eas-ter day with joy was bright; the sun shone out with
2 O Je-sus, king of gen-tle-ness, with con-stant love our
3 O Christ, you are the Lord of all in this our Eas-ter
4 All praise, O ris-en Lord, we give to you, once dead, but

fair-er light, Al-le-lu-ia! Al-le-lu-ia!
hearts pos-sess. Al-le-lu-ia! Al-le-lu-ia!
fes-ti-val, Al-le-lu-ia! Al-le-lu-ia!
now a-live! Al-le-lu-ia! Al-le-lu-ia!

when, to their long-ing eyes re-stored, the a-pos-tles saw
To you our lips will ev-er raise the trib-ute of
for you will be our strength and shield from ev-'ry weap-
To God the Fa-ther e-qual praise, and God the Ho-

their ris-en Lord! Al-le-lu-ia! Al-le-lu-ia!
our grate-ful praise. Al-le-lu-ia! Al-le-lu-ia!
on death can wield. Al-le-lu-ia! Al-le-lu-ia!
ly Ghost, we raise! Al-le-lu-ia! Al-le-lu-ia!

Al-le-lu-ia, al-le-lu-ia, al-le-lu-ia!

Text: Latin hymn, 4th or 5th cent.; tr. John M. Neale, 1818–1866, alt.
Music: LASST UNS ERFREUEN, *Geistliche Kirchengesänge*, Köln, 1623

LASST UNS ERFREUEN is another tune often associated with this ancient Easter hymn, sung for centuries as a morning hymn each day from the Sunday after Easter until Ascension.—(Accompaniment: LBW 143)

The Clouds of Judgment Gather

1 The clouds of judg-ment gath - er; the time is grow-ing late;
2 A - rise, O true dis - ci - ples; let wrong give way to right,
3 The home of fade - less splen - dor, of blooms that bear no thorn,
4 Oh, hap - py, ho - ly por - tion, re - lief for all dis - tressed,

be so - ber and be watch - ful; our judge is at the gate:
and pen - i - ten - tial shad - ow to Je - sus' bless-ed light:
where they shall dwell as chil - dren who here as ex - iles mourn;
true vi - sion of true beau - ty, re - fresh-ment for the blest!

the judge who comes in mer - cy, the judge who comes in might
the light that has no eve - ning, that knows no moon or sun,
the peace of all the faith - ful, the calm of all the blest,
Strive now to win that glo - ry; toil now to gain that light;

to put an end to e - vil and di - a - dem the right.
the light so new and gold - en, the light that is but one.
in - vi - o - late, un - fad - ing, di - vin - est, sweet-est, best.
send hope a - head to grasp it, till hope be lost in sight.

Text: Bernard of Cluny, 12th cent.; tr. *Lutheran Book of Worship*, 1978
Music: KING'S LYNN, English folk tune
Text © 1978 *Lutheran Book of Worship*, admin. Augsburg Fortress

This hymn is an excerpt from a Latin poem of nearly three thousand lines that is also the source for "Jerusalem the golden." Its author lived in the renowned French abbey at Cluny. In addition to the Irish tune with which it is paired in *Lutheran Book of Worship*, it may be sung to this English melody.—(Accompaniment: LBW 428, WOV 647)

The Day of Resurrection!

1 The day of res-ur-rec-tion! Earth, tell it out a-broad,
2 Let hearts be purged of e-vil that we may see a-right
3 Now let the heav'ns be joy-ful, let earth its song be-gin,
4 Then praise we God the Fa-ther, and praise we Christ his Son,

the pass-o-ver of glad-ness, the pass-o-ver of God.
the Lord in rays e-ter-nal of res-ur-rec-tion light,
let all the world keep tri-umph and all that is there-in.
with them the Ho-ly Spir-it, e-ter-nal Three in One;

From death to life e-ter-nal, from sin's do-min-ion free,
and lis-t'ning to his ac-cents, may hear, so calm and plain,
Let all things, seen and un-seen, their notes of glad-ness blend;
till all the ran-somed num-ber fall down be-fore the throne,

our Christ has brought us o-ver with hymns of vic-to-ry.
his own "All hail!" and hear-ing, may raise the vic-tor strain.
for Christ the Lord has ris-en, our joy that has no end!
and hon-or, pow'r, and glo-ry, as-cribe to God a-lone!

Text: John of Damascus, c. 696–c. 754; tr. John M. Neale, 1818–1866, alt.
Music: ELLACOMBE, M. V. Werkmeister, *Gesangbuch der Herzogl. Hofkapelle*, 1784

This ancient hymn celebrating the Easter passover of Christ and the church is widely sung to the two tunes given here.
ELLACOMBE is the common tune name for a melody that is found with the text "Ave Maria, klarer und lichter Morgenstern"
in a collection used in the private chapel of the Duke of Württemberg.—(Accompaniment: LBW 251)

The Day of Resurrection!

1 The day of res - ur - rec - tion! Earth, tell it out a - broad,
2 Let hearts be purged of e - vil that we may see a - right
3 Now let the heav'ns be joy - ful, let earth its song be - gin,
4 Then praise we God the Fa - ther, and praise we Christ his Son,

the pass - o - ver of glad - ness, the pass - o - ver of God.
the Lord in rays e - ter - nal of res - ur - rec - tion light,
let all the world keep tri - umph and all that is there - in.
with them the Ho - ly Spir - it, e - ter - nal Three in One;

From death to life e - ter - nal, from sin's do - min - ion free,
and lis - t'ning to his ac - cents, may hear, so calm and plain,
Let all things, seen and un - seen, their notes of glad - ness blend;
till all the ran - somed num - ber fall down be - fore the throne,

our Christ has brought us o - ver with hymns of vic - to - ry.
his own "All hail!" and hear - ing, may raise the vic - tor strain.
for Christ the Lord has ris - en, our joy that has no end!
and hon - or, pow'r, and glo - ry, as - cribe to God a - lone!

Text: John of Damascus, c. 696–c. 754; tr. John M. Neale, 1818–1866, alt.
Music: LANCASHIRE, Henry T. Smart, 1813–1879

This ancient hymn celebrating the Easter passover of Christ and the church is widely sung to the two tunes given here. LANCASHIRE was originally composed for a large missionary meeting in Blackburn, Lancashire, in 1836, as a setting for "From Greenland's icy mountains."—(Accompaniment: LBW 495)

There's a Wideness in God's Mercy

1 There's a wide-ness in God's mer-cy, like the wide-ness of the sea;
2 There is wel-come for the sin-ner, and a prom-ised grace made good;
3 For the love of God is broad-er than the mea-sures of our mind;
4 'Tis not all we owe to Je-sus; it is some-thing more than all:

there's a kind-ness in his jus-tice which is more than lib-er-ty.
there is mer-cy with the Sav-ior; there is heal-ing in his blood.
and the heart of the e-ter-nal is most won-der-ful-ly kind.
great-er good be-cause of e-vil, larg-er mer-cy through the fall.

There is no place where earth's sor-rows are more felt than up in heav'n.
There is grace e-nough for thou-sands of new worlds as great as this;
There is plen-ti-ful re-demp-tion in the blood that has been shed;
If our love were but more sim-ple, we should take him at his word;

There is no place where earth's fail-ings have such kind-ly judg-ment giv'n.
there is room for fresh cre-a-tions in that up-per home of bliss.
there is joy for all the mem-bers in the sor-rows of the head.
and our lives would be all sun-shine in the sweet-ness of our Lord.

Text: Frederick W. Faber, 1814–1863
Music: BEECHER, John Zundel, 1815–1882

76 BEECHER is a tune often associated with this hymn text. The tune was written in 1870 for "Love divine, all loves excelling" and named for Henry Ward Beecher, pastor of Plymouth Congregational Church in Brooklyn, New York, where the composer was organist at the time.

There's a Wideness in God's Mercy

1. There's a wide-ness in God's mer - cy, like the wide-ness of the sea; there's a kind-ness in his jus-tice which is more than lib - er - ty. There is no place where earth's sor - rows are more felt than up in heav'n. There is no place where earth's fail - ings have such kind - ly judg-ment giv'n.

2. There is wel-come for the sin - ner, and a prom-ised grace made good; there is mer - cy with the Sav - ior; there is heal - ing in his blood. There is grace e - nough for thou-sands of new worlds as great as this; there is room for fresh cre - a - tions in that up - per home of bliss.

3. For the love of God is broad - er than the mea - sures of our mind; and the heart of the e - ter - nal is most won - der - ful - ly kind. There is plen - ti - ful re - demp - tion in the blood that has been shed; there is joy for all the mem - bers in the sor - rows of the head.

4. 'Tis not all we owe to Je - sus; it is some-thing more than all: great - er good be - cause of e - vil, larg - er mer - cy through the fall. If our love were but more sim - ple, we should take him at his word; and our lives would be all sun - shine in the sweet-ness of our Lord.

Text: Frederick W. Faber, 1814–1863

Music: ST. HELENA, Calvin Hampton, 1938–1984

ST. HELENA is another tune more recently associated with Faber's text. Calvin Hampton's flowing accompaniment and an understated melody create a very different environment for the text as compared to the foursquare BEECHER tune.
—(Accompaniment: page 78)

There's a Wideness in God's Mercy

1 There's a wide - ness in God's mer - cy, like the wide - ness
2 There is wel - come for the sin - ner, and a prom - ised
3 For the love of God is broad - er than the mea - sures
4 'Tis not all we owe to Je - sus; it is some - thing

of the sea; there's a kind - ness in his jus -
grace made good; there is mer - cy with the Sav -
of our mind; and the heart of the e - ter -
more than all: great - er good be - cause of e -

tice which is more than lib - er - ty. There is no place
ior; there is heal - ing in his blood. There is grace e -
nal is most won - der - ful - ly kind. There is plen - ti -
vil, larg - er mer - cy through the fall. If our love were

where earth's sor-rows / are more felt than up in heav'n.There is no place
nough for thou-sands / of new worlds as great as this; there is room for
ful re-demp-tion / in the blood that has been shed; there is joy for
but more sim-ple, / we should take him at his word; and our lives would

where earth's fail - ings / have such kind - ly judg-ment giv'n.
fresh cre - a - tions / in that up - per home of bliss.
all the mem - bers / in the sor - rows of the head.
be all sun - shine / in the sweet-ness of our Lord.

Text: Frederick W. Faber, 1814–1863

Music: ST. HELENA, Calvin Hampton, 1938–1984

Music © 1977 GIA Publications Inc., 7404 S. Mason Ave., Chicago IL 60638, (800) 442-1358. All rights reserved.

ST. HELENA is another tune more recently associated with Faber's text. Calvin Hampton's flowing accompaniment and an understated melody create a very different environment for the text as compared to the foursquare BEECHER tune.

They Cast Their Nets

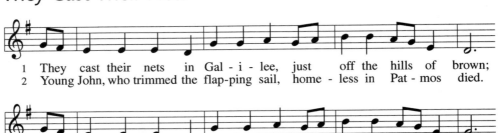

1 They cast their nets in Gal - i - lee, just off the hills of brown;
2 Young John, who trimmed the flap-ping sail, home - less in Pat - mos died.

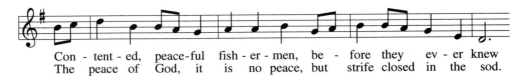

such hap - py, peace-ful fish - er - folk be - fore the Lord came down.
Pe - ter, who hauled the teem-ing net, head down was cru - ci - fied.

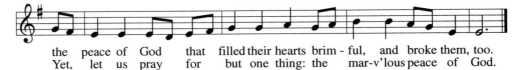

Con - tent - ed, peace-ful fish - er - men, be - fore they ev - er knew
The peace of God, it is no peace, but strife closed in the sod.

the peace of God that filled their hearts brim - ful, and broke them, too.
Yet, let us pray for but one thing: the mar-v'lous peace of God.

Text: William A. Percy, 1885–1942
Music: KINGSFOLD, English melody
Text © The Goodman Group, 254 W. 54th St., New York NY 10022, (212) 246-3333. All rights reserved.

"His Peace," from *Enzio's Kingdom and Other Poems*, is the work by Southern poet William Alexander Percy from which this hymn is derived. Pairing it with an accessible tune like KINGSFOLD may increase its use.—(Accompaniment: WOV 730)

This Is the Spirit's Entry Now

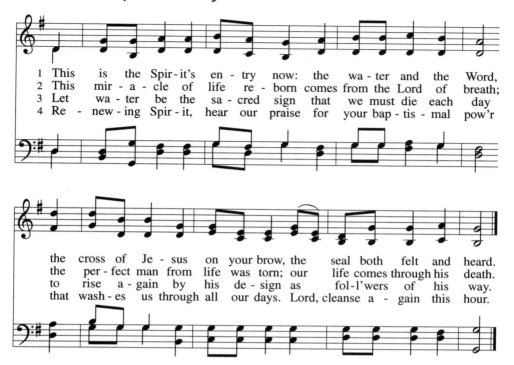

1 This is the Spir-it's en-try now: the wa-ter and the Word,
2 This mir-a-cle of life re-born comes from the Lord of breath;
3 Let wa-ter be the sa-cred sign that we must die each day
4 Re-new-ing Spir-it, hear our praise for your bap-tis-mal pow'r

the cross of Je-sus on your brow, the seal both felt and heard.
the per-fect man from life was torn; our life comes through his death.
to rise a-gain by his de-sign as fol-l'wers of his way.
that wash-es us through all our days. Lord, cleanse a-gain this hour.

Text: Thomas E. Herbranson, b. 1933, alt.

Music: AZMON, Carl G. Gläser, 1784–1829

Text © Thomas E. Herbranson, admin. Augsburg Fortress

This baptismal text was first published in the provisional materials that preceded *Lutheran Book of Worship.* AZMON is a common tune, known from its association with "Oh, for a thousand tongues to sing," which carries the text well.

Wake, Awake, for Night Is Flying

1 Wake, a - wake, for night is fly - ing, the watch-men
2 Zi - on hears the watch-men sing - ing, and all her
3 Glo - ri - a! Let heav'n a - dore you! Let saints and

on the heights are cry - ing; a - wake, Je - ru - sa - lem, at last.
heart with joy is spring-ing. She wakes, she ris - es from her gloom.
an - gels sing be - fore you, with harp and cym - bal's clear-est tone.

Mid - night hears the wel - come voic - es, and at the
Her dear friend comes down, all glo - rious, the strong in
Gates of pearl, twelve por - tals gleam - ing, lead us to

thrill-ing cry re - joic - es: "Come forth, you maid-ens! Night is past.
grace, in truth vic - to - rious: her star is ris'n; her light is come.
bliss be - yond all dream - ing, with an - gel choirs a - round your throne.

The bride-groom comes! A - wake; your lamps with glad - ness take!"
Now come, O Bless - ed One, Lord Je - sus, God's own Son.
No eye has caught the light, no ear the thun - 'd'ring might

Al - le - lu - ia! Rise and pre - pare the feast to
Sing ho - san - na! Oh, hear the call! Come one, come
of such glo - ry. There we will go: what joy we'll

share; go, meet the bride - groom, who draws near.
all, and fol - low to the ban - quet hall.
know! There sweet de - light will ev - er flow.

Text: Philipp Nicolai, 1556–1608; tr. Catherine Winkworth, 1829–1878, and Martin A. Seltz, b. 1951

Music: WACHET AUF, Philipp Nicolai, 1556–1608

Text © 1999 Augsburg Fortress

Sometimes called the "king of chorales," this hymn is filled with images fitting for the last days of the church year and the first days of Advent. This version offers a composite translation based on Catherine Winkworth's, which allows much of the spirit and sound of the original to shine through. This rhythmic version of the melody matches the current standard in German hymnals.—(Accompaniment: LBW 31)

We Are Turning, Lord, to Hear You

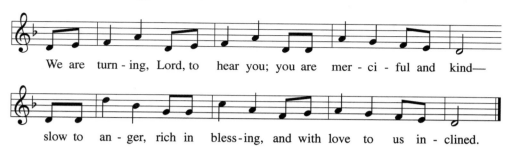

We are turn-ing, Lord, to hear you; you are mer-ci-ful and kind—
slow to an-ger, rich in bless-ing, and with love to us in-clined.

Text: metrical Lenten acclamation based on Joel 2:13, Gracia Grindal, b. 1943
Music: KAS DZIEDAJA, Latvian folk tune
Text © 1998 Augsburg Fortress

Permission is granted for congregations to reproduce this hymn between July 1, 2001, and December 31, 2005, provided copies are for local use only and the following copyright notice appears: From *Congregational Song: Proposals for Renewal,* © 2001, admin. Augsburg Fortress.

Precedent for metrical paraphrases of liturgical texts reaches back before the Reformation to the medieval *leisen.* This text was part of a hymn mass commissioned for *Sundays and Seasons.* Paraphrases of the principal recurring portions of the eucharistic liturgy comprise the hymn mass texts, which can be sung to a variety of common tunes.—(Accompaniment: WOV 656)

We Plow the Fields
Aramos nuestros campos

1 We plow the fields and scat-ter the good seed on the land,
1 A - ra-mos nues-tros cam-pos, y lue-go_el sem-bra - dor

but it is fed and wa-tered by God's al-might-y hand.
en e-llos la si - mien-te es-par-ce con a - mor.

God sends the snow in win-ter, the warmth to swell the grain,
Mas es de Dios la ma-no que la_ha-ce ger-mi - nar,

the breez-es and the sun-shine, and soft re-fresh-ing rain.
ca-lor y llu-via dan-do a to-dos por i - gual.

Text: Matthias Claudius, 1740–1815, tr. Jane M. Campbell, 1817–1878 (English, alt.), and Ernesto Barocio (Spanish)

Music: San Fernando, Luis Olivieri, b. 1937

We Plow the Fields
Aramos nuestros campos

1 We plow the fields and scat-ter the good seed on the land,
1 A - ra - mos nues-tros cam-pos, y lue - go_el sem-bra - dor

but it is fed and wa-tered by God's al - might-y hand.
en e - llos la si - mien-te es - par - ce con a - mor.

God sends the snow in win - ter, the warmth to swell the grain,
Mas es de Dios la ma - no que la_ha - ce ger - mi - nar,

the breez-es and the sun - shine, and soft re - fresh-ing rain.
ca - lor y llu - via dan - do a to - dos por i - gual.

2 You only are the maker
of all things near and far.
You paint the wayside flower,
you light the evening star.
The winds and waves obey you,
by you the birds are fed;
much more to us, your children,
you give our daily bread.

2 El hacedor supremo
de cuanto existe es él.
Su aroma da a las flores
y a las abejas miel.
Las aves alimenta,
de peces puebla el mar,
y da a las gentes todas
el cotidiano pan.

3 We thank you, our creator,
for all things bright and good,
the seed-time and the harvest,
our life, our health, our food.
The gifts we have to offer
are what your love imparts
and, what you most would treasure,
our humble, thankful hearts.

3 Mil gracias, Dios, te damos
por cuanto bien nos das:
las flores y los frutos,
salud, la vida y pan.
No hay con qué paguemos
lo que nos da tu amor,
más que nuestro sincero
y humilde corazón.

Text: Matthias Claudius, 1740–1815, tr. Jane M. Campbell, 1817–1878 (English, alt.), and Ernesto Barocio (Spanish)

Music: SAN FERNANDO, Luis Olivieri, b. 1937

Claudius was an eighteenth century German poet who wrote this text as part of a sketch depicting a harvest-thanksgiving celebration. Translated into English by a London music teacher (here with some minor alterations to minimize masculine language) and more recently into Spanish, it is here set to the melody with which it appears in *Libro de Liturgia y Cántico*. It is an example of a classic text finding new life in the context of another language and musical idiom.

What God Ordains Is Good Indeed

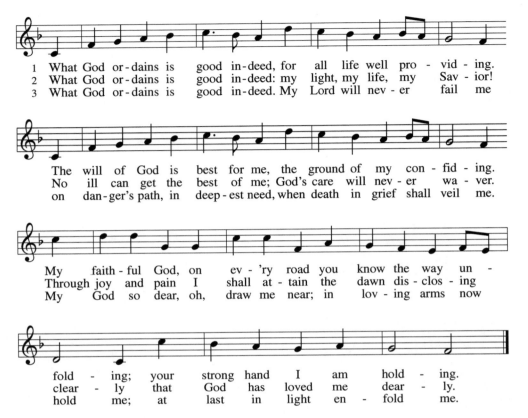

1 What God or-dains is good in-deed, for all life well pro - vid - ing.
2 What God or-dains is good in-deed: my light, my life, my Sav - ior!
3 What God or-dains is good in-deed. My Lord will nev - er fail me

The will of God is best for me, the ground of my con - fid - ing.
No ill can get the best of me; God's care will nev - er wa - ver.
on dan-ger's path, in deep-est need, when death in grief shall veil me.

My faith - ful God, on ev - 'ry road you know the way un -
Through joy and pain I shall at - tain the dawn dis - clos - ing
My God so dear, oh, draw me near; in lov - ing arms now

fold - ing; your strong hand I am hold - ing.
clear - ly that God has loved me dear - ly.
hold me; at last in light en - fold me.

Text: Samuel Rodigast, 1649–1708; tr. Martin A. Seltz, b. 1951
Music: WAS GOTT TUT, attr. Severus Gastorius, 1646–1682

Text © 2000 Augsburg Fortress

A new translation was undertaken for this text, cast primarily in the second person to capture the sense of intimacy in the original. The hymn was written by Rodigast to console the author's friend, the composer Gastorius, during a time of illness. The rhythm of the original last line of the tune is reflected in this version.—(Accompaniment: LBW 446)

When Christ's Appearing Was Made Known

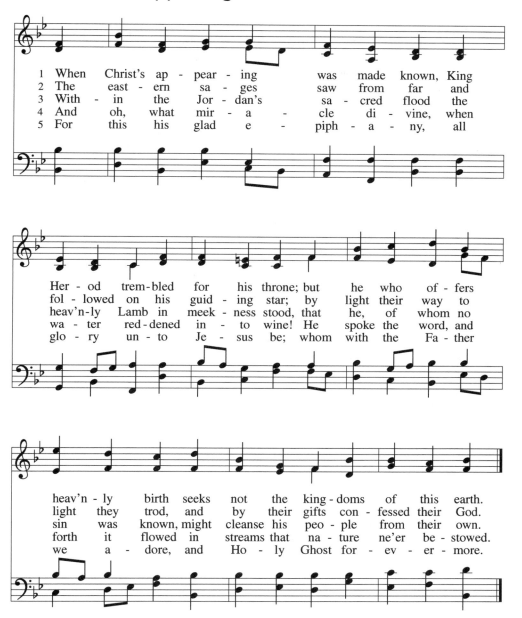

1 When Christ's ap - pear - ing was made known, King
2 The east - ern sa - ges saw from far and
3 With - in the Jor - dan's sa - cred flood the
4 And oh, what mir - a - cle di - vine, when
5 For this his glad e - piph - a - ny, all

Her - od trem-bled for his throne; but he who of - fers
fol - lowed on his guid - ing star; by light their way to
heav'n-ly Lamb in meek - ness stood, that he, of whom no
wa - ter red-dened in - to wine! He spoke the word, and
glo - ry un - to Je - sus be; whom with the Fa - ther

heav'n - ly birth seeks not the king - doms of this earth.
light they trod, and by their gifts con - fessed their God.
sin was known, might cleanse his peo - ple from their own.
forth it flowed in streams that na - ture ne'er be - stowed.
we a - dore, and Ho - ly Ghost for - ev - er - more.

Text: Coelius Sedulius, c. 5th cent.; tr. composite
Music: WINCHESTER NEW, Georg Wittwe's *Musikalisch Handbuch,* 1690

One of the oldest Epiphany hymns, this text is the continuation of the Christmas hymn "From east to west, from shore to shore" in *Lutheran Book of Worship* (no. 64). WINCHESTER NEW is a common tune that may be used to carry this useful text that refers to the three major signs of Christ's revealing: the guiding star, the baptism in the Jordan, and the miracle of the wine at the wedding in Cana.

When I Survey the Wondrous Cross

1 When I sur - vey the won - drous cross on which the prince of glo - ry died, my rich - est gain I count but loss and pour con - tempt on all my pride.

2 For - bid it, Lord, that I should boast save in the death of Christ, my God; all the vain things that charm me most, I sac - ri - fice them to his blood.

3 See, from his head, his hands, his feet, sor - row and love flow min - gled down. Did e'er such love and sor - row meet, or thorns com - pose so rich a crown?

4 Were the whole realm of na - ture mine, that were a trib - ute far too small; love so a - maz - ing, so di - vine, de - mands my soul, my life, my all.

Text: Isaac Watts, 1674–1748
Music: HAMBURG, Lowell Mason, 1792–1872

This combination of text and tune has widespread ecumenical acceptance. Lowell Mason, a preeminent hymnologist and music educator in nineteenth century New England, based the tune on tone 1 of Gregorian plainsong.

When Peace, like a River

1 When peace, like a riv-er, at-tend-eth my way; when
2 Though Sa-tan should buf-fet, though tri-als should come, let
3 He lives—oh, the bliss of this glo-ri-ous thought; my
4 And Lord, haste the day when our faith shall be sight, the

sor-rows, like sea bil-lows, roll; what-ev-er my lot, thou hast
this blest as-sur-ance con-trol, that Christ hath re-gard-ed my
sin, not in part, but the whole, is nailed to his cross and I
clouds be rolled back as a scroll, the trum-pet shall sound and the

taught me to say, it is well, it is well with my soul.
help-less es-tate, and hath shed his own blood for my soul.
bear it no more. Praise the Lord, praise the Lord, O, my soul!
Lord shall de-scend; e-ven so it is well with my soul.

Refrain

It is well with my soul, it is well, it is well with my soul.
it is well with my soul,

Text: Horatio G. Spafford, 1828–1888
Music: VILLE DU HAVRE, Philip P. Bliss, 1838–1876

This hymn was written by Spafford in the aftermath of an accident at sea involving the S.S. *Ville du Havre*, which took the lives of his four daughters. This version restores to the hymn its popular refrain, which was omitted from *Lutheran Book of Worship*.

Where True Charity and Love Abide
Ubi caritas

In ho - ly won - der let us love the liv - ing God,
Con - ten - tion, en - vy, ill will, spite, may these all cease;
With ho - ly joy far be - yond thought we shall be full,

Refrain

and may our hearts ev - er be one in faith - ful love.
with us, a - bid - ing in our midst, is Christ our God.
from age to age, world with-out end, for - ev - er - more.

Text: Latin, 9th cent.; tr. composite

Music: UBI CARITAS, plainsong, mode 6, arr. Richard Proulx, b. 1937

Text © 1995, 2001 Augsburg Fortress

This Latin hymn has long been associated with the liturgy of Maundy Thursday, where it is used to accompany the washing of feet. A metrical paraphrase of the text appears in *Lutheran Book of Worship* (no. 126) to an American melody. This version uses the original and very singable chant melody and a close translation of the original Latin words.

Where True Charity and Love Abide
Ubi caritas

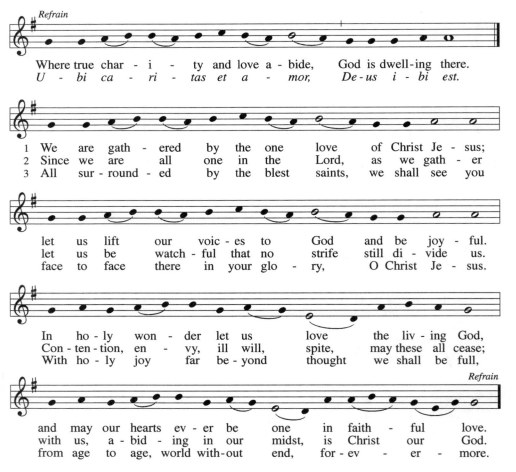

Refrain

Where true char - i - ty and love a - bide, God is dwell-ing there.
U - bi ca - ri - tas et a - mor, De-us i - bi est.

1 We are gath - ered by the one love of Christ Je - sus;
2 Since we are all one in the Lord, as we gath - er
3 All sur - round - ed by the blest saints, we shall see you

let us lift our voic - es to God and be joy - ful.
let us be watch - ful that no strife still di - vide us.
face to face there in your glo - ry, O Christ Je - sus.

In ho - ly won - der let us love the liv - ing God,
Con - ten - tion, en - vy, ill will, spite, may these all cease;
With ho - ly joy far be - yond thought we shall be full,

Refrain

and may our hearts ev - er be one in faith - ful love.
with us, a - bid - ing in our midst, is Christ our God.
from age to age, world with-out end, for - ev - er - more.

Text: Latin, 9th cent.; tr. composite
Music: UBI CARITAS, plainsong, mode 6
Text © 1995, 2001 Augsburg Fortress

Permission is granted for congregations to reproduce this hymn between July 1, 2001, and December 31, 2005, provided copies are for local use only and the following copyright notice appears: From *Congregational Song: Proposals for Renewal*, © 2001, admin. Augsburg Fortress.

This Latin hymn has long been associated with the liturgy of Maundy Thursday, where it is used to accompany the washing of feet. A metrical paraphrase of the text appears in *Lutheran Book of Worship* (no. 126) to an American melody. This version uses the original and very singable chant melody and a close translation of the original Latin words.

Indexes

Worship Book Reference Index

For comparison and reference, this index notes parallels to the contents of *Congregational Song: Proposals for Renewal*, as they appear in the following service books and hymnals:

LBW: Lutheran Book of Worship
LLC: Libro de Liturgia y Cántico
SBH: Service Book and Hymnal
TLH: The Lutheran Hymnal
TFF: This Far by Faith
WOV: With One Voice

Tune Index

Title Index

Evaluation

An essential goal of Renewing Worship is the evaluation of proposed strategies for renewal by worshiping congregations and their leaders. Included here as well as at www.renewingworship.org is a reproducible evaluation tool that addresses *Congregational Song: Proposals for Renewal.* Feedback received will help to shape the subsequent stages of the process toward new worship materials.

Renewal of Texts

Strategy: Recovering biblical and poetic imagery
Examples: God Is Truly Present; In Peace and Joy I Now Depart; Praise to the Lord, the Almighty; Savior of the Nations, Come; Wake, Awake, for Night Is Flying

	Inappropriate			Appropriate
This strategy is:	1		2	3

	Unsuccessful				Successful
Examples of this strategy are:	1	2	3	4	5

Comments:

Strategy: Restoring older texts and translations
Examples: All My Heart This Night Rejoices; Behold a Host; From Heaven Above to Earth I Come; I Love to Tell the Story; In the Bleak Midwinter; Lo, How a Rose E'er Blooming

	Inappropriate			Appropriate
This strategy is:	1		2	3

	Unsuccessful				Successful
Examples of this strategy are:	1	2	3	4	5

Comments:

Strategy: *Introducing new texts and translations*

Examples: All Creatures, Worship God Most High; Day of Arising; Rise, O Church, like Christ Arisen; Sing Praise to God, Who Has Shaped; What God Ordains Is Good Indeed

	Inappropriate		Appropriate
This strategy is:	1	2	3

	Unsuccessful				Successful
Examples of this strategy are:	1	2	3	4	5

Comments:

Strategy: *Offering an ecumenical text or version of a text*

Examples: Creator of the Stars of Night; Hail the Day That Sees Him Rise; Lift Up Your Heads, Ye Mighty Gates; Lo, How a Rose E'er Blooming; My Shepherd, You Supply My Need

	Inappropriate		Appropriate
This strategy is:	1	2	3

	Unsuccessful				Successful
Examples of this strategy are:	1	2	3	4	5

Comments:

Strategy: Using expansive language for God and humanity
Examples: Ah, Holy Jesus; A Mighty Fortress Is Our God; Faith of Our Fathers; In Christ There Is No East or West; Praise, My Soul, the God of Heaven; Sing Praise to God, Who Has Shaped

	Inappropriate		Appropriate
This strategy is:	1	2	3

	Unsuccessful				Successful
Examples of this strategy are:	1	2	3	4	5

Comments:

Renewal of Music

Strategy: Restoring older tunes for selected texts
Examples: All My Heart This Night Rejoices; Come, Thou Long Expected Jesus; Ride On, Ride On in Majesty; Savior, like a Shepherd Lead Us; When I Survey the Wondrous Cross

	Inappropriate		Appropriate
This strategy is:	1	2	3

	Unsuccessful				Successful
Examples of this strategy are:	1	2	3	4	5

Comments:

Strategy: *Introducing common tunes for selected texts*

Examples: Christ Is the King!; God Loved the World; I Heard the Voice of Jesus Say; In His Temple Now Behold Him; O Blessed Spring; The Day of Resurrection; This Is the Spirit's Entry Now; When Christ's Appearing Was Made Known

	Inappropriate		Appropriate
This strategy is:	1	2	3

	Unsuccessful				Successful
Examples of this strategy are:	1	2	3	4	5

Comments:

Strategy: *Offering an ecumenical tune or version of a tune*

Examples: A Stable Lamp Is Lighted; Hark! A Thrilling Voice Is Sounding!; I Heard the Voice of Jesus Say; That Easter Day with Joy Was Bright; The Day of Resurrection

	Inappropriate		Appropriate
This strategy is:	1	2	3

	Unsuccessful				Successful
Examples of this strategy are:	1	2	3	4	5

Comments:

Strategy: *Introducing broadened musical styles and traditions*
Examples: Aramos nuestros; Deep River; For the Bread Which You Have Broken

	Inappropriate		Appropriate
This strategy is:	1	2	3

	Unsuccessful				Successful
Examples of this strategy are:	1	2	3	4	5

Comments:

Strategy: *Encouraging unison or harmony singing as appropriate*
Examples: A Mighty Fortress Is Our God; Amazing Grace, How Sweet the Sound; Lift Every Voice and Sing; O Sacred Head, Now Wounded; Restore in Us, O God; When I Survey the Wondrous Cross

	Inappropriate		Appropriate
This strategy is:	1	2	3

	Unsuccessful				Successful
Examples of this strategy are:	1	2	3	4	5

Comments:

General comments:

Do Polar Bears Snooze in Hollow Trees?

A Book About Animal Hibernation

by Laura Purdie Salas

illustrated by Todd Ouren

PICTURE WINDOW BOOKS
Minneapolis, Minnesota

Special thanks to our advisers for their expertise:

Zoological Society of San Diego
San Diego Zoo, San Diego, California

Susan Kesselring, M.A., Literacy Educator
Rosemount–Apple Valley–Eagan (Minnesota) School District

Editor: Christianne Jones
Designer: Nathan Gassman
Page Production: Melissa Kes
Creative Director: Keith Griffin
Editorial Director: Carol Jones
The illustrations in this book were created digitally.

Picture Window Books
5115 Excelsior Boulevard
Suite 232
Minneapolis, MN 55416
877-845-8392
www.picturewindowbooks.com

Printed in the United States of America.

Library of Congress Cataloging-in-Publication Data
Salas, Laura Purdie.
Do polar bears snooze in hollow trees? : a book about animal hibernation /
by Laura Purdie Salas ; illustrated by Todd Ouren.
p. cm. — (Animals all around)
Includes bibliographical references.
ISBN-13: 978-1-4048-2231-3 (hardcover)
ISBN-10: 1-4048-2231-3 (hardcover)
1. Hibernation—Juvenile literature. I. Ouren, Todd, ill. II. Title. III. Series.

QL755.S25 2007
591.56'5—dc22
2006003588

Editor's Note: There is often more than one species of each animal. The hibernation habits
described in this book are a general overview of each animal, unless a specific species is noted.

Do polar bears hang from the ceiling?

No! Bats hang from the ceiling.

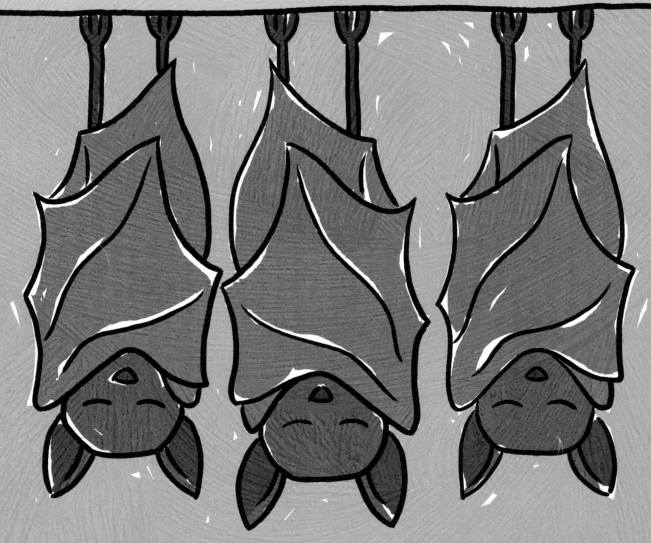

Bats crowd together on cave ceilings and walls. They cluster so closely together that several hundred bats can fit in 1 square foot (.09 square meters). They may lose up to half their body weight while they sleep through the winter.

Do polar bears burrow
in the mud?

No! Carp burrow in the mud.

In the fall, a carp beats its tail on the muddy pond bottom to bury itself. Its heartbeat slows down, and it falls deeply asleep. It hibernates in its warm, muddy bed all winter. In the spring, the ice on the pond melts, and the carp wakes up.

Do polar bears snooze in hollow trees?

No! Raccoons snooze in hollow trees.

Raccoons doze all winter in small groups inside hollow trees. They sleep more lightly than many animals in true hibernation. On warm days, they even wander out into the sunshine. After they snack on plants or bugs, raccoons crawl back into the tree to snooze some more.

Do polar bears crowd
into wiggling balls?

No! Snakes crowd into wiggling balls.

When the air turns chilly, a garter snake's body temperature drops. But these cold-blooded animals know how to stay warm. Garter snakes gather in huge balls underground to keep each other warm.

Do polar bears turn into ice?

No! Frogs turn into ice.

Each winter, almost one half of the water in a wood frog's body freezes. The frog turns into a frozen block. Its heart and brain completely stop. When spring comes, the wood frog thaws and starts hopping again.

Do polar bears stay underground most of the year?

No! Gila monsters stay underground most of the year.

Gila monsters are large lizards that live in the desert. They spend 98 percent of their lives underground. In the summer, they stay underground to avoid the hot sun. In the winter, they hibernate. They live off the fat stored in their tails.

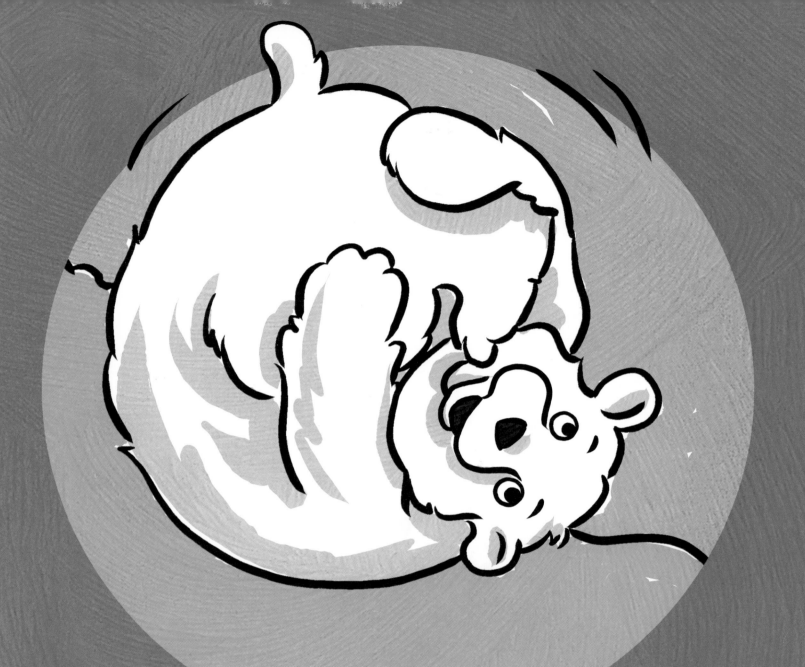

Do polar bears curl up
in tiny balls?

No! Squirrels curl up in tiny balls.

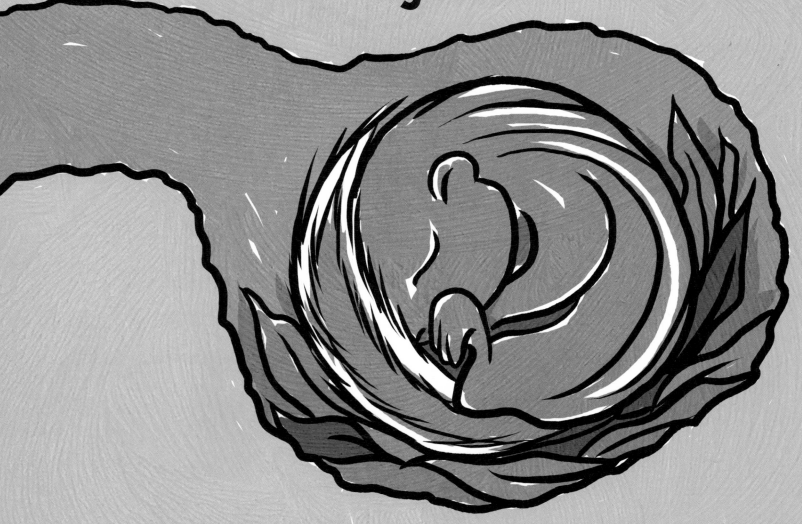

During the fall, a ground squirrel gobbles seeds and bugs. The squirrel gains weight to help it survive the winter. Then it curls up in its underground den. It tucks its tail around its head and falls asleep.

Do polar bears sleep
through the summer?

17

No! Crocodiles sleep through the summer.

In very hot regions, crocodiles sleep through the summer. Small ponds disappear during the dry season. Crocodiles burrow into the ground or rest below a shoreline ledge. They sleep until the rains return to refill the ponds.

Do polar bears breathe
through mud?

No! Turtles breathe through mud.

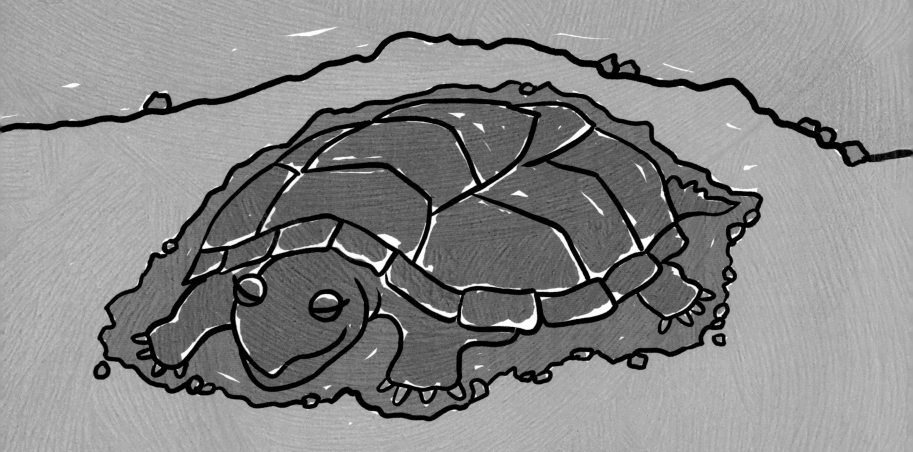

For half of the year, snapping turtles stick their heads above water to breathe air. During the other half of the year, snapping turtles hibernate deep in the mud. Their body temperature plunges, and they lie very still. They breathe air that is trapped in the mud.

Do polar bears sleep
in snow caves?

Yes! Polar bears sleep in snow caves.

All polar bears sleep
in the snow, but only a pregnant polar bear hibernates.
She digs her den under the snow in the fall. She makes
two separate rooms and climbs in. In the winter, she
gives birth to two tiny cubs. She spends the rest of the
winter in one room, and the cubs share the other room.

Where Animals Hibernate

Some animals hibernate in cozy spots.

· · · · · · · · · · · ·Raccoons find empty trees.

Polar bears make snow caves. ·

Some animals hibernate underground.

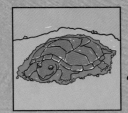

Carp burrow in the mud. ·

· · · · · · · Turtles dig into the mud.

Squirrels curl up underground. ·

· · · · · · · Gila monsters spend 98 percent of their lives underground.

Some animals hibernate in surprising ways.

· · · · · · · · · · · ·Crocodiles sleep through the hot, dry season.

Snakes keep each other warm in a big ball.· · · · · · · ·

· · · · · · ·Frogs freeze solid.

Bats hang on cave ceilings. ·

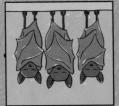

Glossary

burrow—a hole or tunnel in the ground made by an animal

cold-blooded—an animal that cannot make its own heat

den—a place where some animals sleep

hibernation—the act of deep sleep or rest during the winter

hollow—having a hole or empty space inside

thaw—to become unfrozen

To Learn More

At the Library

Crossingham, John and Bobbie Kalman. *What Is Hibernation?* New York: Crabtree Publishing, 2002.

Ganeri, Anita. *Hibernation.* Portsmouth, N.H.: Heinemann Library, 2005.

Wallace, Karen. *A Bed for the Winter.* New York: Dorling Kindersley, 2001.

On the Web

FactHound offers a safe, fun way to find Internet sites related to this book. All of the sites on FactHound have been researched by our staff.

1. Visit *www.facthound.com*
2. Type in this special code for age-appropriate sites: 1404822313
3. Click on the FETCH IT button.

Your trusty FactHound will fetch the best sites for you!

Index

Look for all of the books in the Animals All Around series:

Do Bears Buzz? A Book About Animal Sounds
    1-4048-0100-6
Do Bees Make Butter? A Book About Things Animals Make
    1-4048-0288-6
Do Cows Eat Cake? A Book About What Animals Eat
    1-4048-0101-4
Do Crocodiles Dance? A Book About Animal Habits
    1-4048-2230-5
Do Dogs Make Dessert? A Book About How Animals Help Humans
    1-4048-0289-4
Do Ducks Live in the Desert? A Book About Where Animals Live
    1-4048-0290-8
Do Frogs Have Fur? A Book About Animal Coats and Coverings
    1-4048-0292-4
Do Goldfish Gallop? A Book About Animal Movement
    1-4048-0105-7
Do Lobsters Leap Waterfalls? A Book About Animal Migration
    1-4048-2234-8
Do Parrots Have Pillows? A Book About Where Animals Sleep
    1-4048-0104-9
Do Pelicans Sip Nectar? A Book About How Animals Eat
    1-4048-2233-X
Do Penguins Have Puppies? A Book About Animal Babies
    1-4048-0102-2
Do Polar Bears Snooze in Hollow trees? A Book About Animal Hibernation
    1-4048-2231-3
Do Salamanders Spit? A Book About How Animals Protect Themselves
    1-4048-0291-6
Do Squirrels Swarm? A Book About Animal Groups
    1-4048-0287-8
Do Turtles Sleep in Treetops? A Book About Animal Homes
    1-4048-2232-1
Do Whales Have Wings? A Book About Animal Bodies
    1-4048-0103-0
Does an Elephant Fit in Your Hand? A Book About Animal Sizes
    1-4048-2235-6